François de Fénelon

Quegli che vince e non colui che perde

Not he who loses but who gains his prize
—Dante, *Inferno*, Canto XV

François de Salignac de La Mothe Fénelon

François de Fénelon

STUDY OF A PERSONALITY

KATHARINE DAY LITTLE

New York

HARPER & BROTHERS PUBLISHERS

Contents

Foreword

In this book I am attempting to show François de Fénelon as a living personality in his place in the France of the seventeenth century. I am writing for all those who cherish acquaintance with stanch and valiant characters, sensitive and gifted souls, in the hope that their lives will be enriched by a knowledge of one more man of such caliber.

As we are aware through our "dreams before midnight and visions out of the ivory gate," there exist many mansions in the house of the Lord, so in the garden of spiritual beauty there pushes up an immense variety of living bloom. To be lovely and enduring, growth in beauty is a necessity; static beauty is never the loftiest. Flowing and flowering must be both concomitant and symbiotic.

As in the natural, so in the spiritual world: the searchers, the seekers, the partially illumined, those possessing, like Fénelon, *plutôt les pennes que les ailes,* the bringers of the necessary and salutary beauty of their own natures to the Throne of all Beauty, these are found no less among the complicated and subtle natures than among the simple and untutored. There are the tortured and solitary shapes, those whose spirits throw out long errant tendrils, wandering from the accepted faith and from the settled conditions of the established order. It is they especially who constitute the experimenters, the givers, the bringers of light, the radicals of the spirit, in a word, the mystics—for, as Charles Bennett has said, whatever of permanent Good will eventually remain, will have been founded on what they have brought to and from the hearts of men throughout the ages. This fact, this process must be a growing developing one, flowing, revealing, finally flowering into the eternal perfection.

Not beside the towering figures of Augustine and Teresa and even the man of Assisi, but in a different rank standing on the edge of a shadow yet alive with his own spiritual incandescence stands the enigmatic, courageous and lovable personality of François de Fénelon, Archbishop of Cambrai.

Many of the translations from the French in both letters and writings have been made by the author.

KATHARINE DAY LITTLE

Boston
Fall, 1950

Acknowledgments

In working upon the study of François de Fénelon, I have been greatly helped by various understanding and sympathetic historians, librarians and scholars. I should like to acknowledge my special gratitude to the staff of the Boston Athenaeum, particularly to Walter Muir Whitehill and David McKibbin; also to Frederick Adams, Curator of the Morgan Library, New York City, who found for me the little-known engraving of Fénelon used in this book. Professors André Morize and T. M. Gilmore of Harvard guided my steps in reading. René Talamon and the late Dewitt H. Parker of the University of Michigan very kindly advised me as to French local color and the correct meaning of dubious phrases. H. Floyd Flewelling of the University of Maine and Professor John H. Randall, Jr. of Columbia have also offered useful suggestions. Elizabeth Boulger has been most useful as well.

It is with sorrow that I speak of the two people who perhaps had most to do, in very different ways, with the writing of this book. My dear friend the late Mildred Whitney Stillman first directed my attention, through her fine translations of his *Spiritual Letters,* to the pure and delicate spirit of Fénelon, to which her own felt a sincere response. By these sympathetic transla-

Acknowledgments

tions she led me to a deeper interest in him, and in the course of writing we often consulted together with perfect unity of feeling about our common subject. The humor, wisdom and long literary experience of William Rose Benét, together with his unfailing warm-hearted interest and willingness to take infinite pains in helping a beginning biographer, have been invaluable to me.

Lastly, my work would never have been accomplished had it not been for the faithful and tireless help given me by my friend Eliza Warren Reed. Quickly won over by the charm and spiritual strength of Fénelon, she has labored valiantly with me over manuscript and notes. Elizabeth Fenn, also an ardent *fénelonien*, and the editor of a collection of his letters, one in the series of *Advent Papers* (Church of the Advent, Boston), was extremely helpful through her industry and appreciation. A word of sincere thanks is also due to Pearl Crist Hall, for her work on the manuscript in its final stages, and especially in clarifying Fénelon's influence on the Quaker movement.

My devoted thanks are owing to one and all.

François de Fénelon

Direction

FRANÇOIS DE SALIGNAC DE LA MOTHE-FÉNELON chose the heart of Périgord in southwest France as his native soil. Now, as in that day, this land of steep hills and pleasant valleys, of poplar and willow groves leading into deep forests, combines wild charm and cultivated country seats. "Truth is more supple on the banks of the Dordogne," says a witty Frenchman, and perhaps this river, which knew such variety of scenery and of folk life, had some subtle part in contributing to Fénelon's penchant for seeing every side of a question. Ronsard, the great sixteenth-century poet and innovator in the development of the French language, sang of the green pleasantness of summer evenings on the Dordogne. Montaigne found the countryside so desirable that at the age of thirty-seven he retired to his father's chateau for life.

Fields of tobacco, rye, and millet fringe the city of Périgueux.

The cathedral of Périgueux, the only Roman-Byzantine church in France, is still an object of animated discussion among architects and archaeologists. Its main part in the form of a Greek cross is thought to date from the thirteenth century and in shape is strongly reminiscent of St. Mark's in Venice, while the Roman façade carries its origin back into imperial days. But Périgueux has other charms besides unique architecture and romantic site. In Périgord, the saying is, everyone is both cook and gourmet. A family preserves the familiar recipes of former days. In the tiniest hamlet the peasant enjoys truffles in his omelet, or revels in them as they burst smoking from the roast turkey before the big fireplace where the knotted vine shoots blaze up. In season a delicious aroma arises from the baskets of fruits, nuts, and mushrooms in the market.

Sarlat is, at present, an unimportant town, but it has a record as an intellectual center. Founded in the twelfth century, it boasted the great medieval scholar, Jean Tarde, who corresponded with Galileo. The publicist, Etienne de La Boétie, friend of Montaigne, was born there. It also made its mark during the religious wars by beating off the Catholic Leaguers. The whole country is now covered with abandoned farms and manors, bearing testimony to the popular complaint of the seventeenth century that farmers were taking to the cities. Auche, another former chief city of the region, is now a *ville morte*. South of Périgueux and Sarlat lies Bergerac, home of the deathless Cyrano. Dumas, too, crowds close, marshaling the shades of his musketeers with the scarlet fox-faced figure of

their deadly enemy, Cardinal Richelieu, in the shadow behind
them.

In the middle of the seventeenth century the family of La
Mothe-Fénelon lived in this countryside. They possessed neither
great offices nor large estates, yet they were allied to many important names. The Gontaut-Biron, the de Gaumont, the de La
Roche-Aymon, de Cadaillac, de Montmorency were of their
kin, and their lineage, said to trace back to the tenth century,
was celebrated in both war and diplomacy.

The best remembered figure among the ancestors of François
de Fénelon is an earlier Marquis de Fénelon, Bertrand, who
acted as ambassador to the court of Queen Elizabeth of England.
He was once asked by his king to draw up a document "putting
the Massacre of St. Bartholomew in the best possible light."
Some of the independence of his descendant is evident in his
answer, although he expressed himself more bluntly than was
the habit of the latter. "Sire, you should have given this task to
those responsible." The ambassador possessed a distinguished
list of correspondents: Catherine de' Medici and Mary Stuart,
Charles IX and Henry III. On April 17, 1571, we find him
writing from London to the queen mother in Paris to tell her
that Signor Cavalcanti would recount the success of his voyage
but in the meanwhile begging her to weigh carefully the matter
in question. The ways of kings and courts were not unknown
to the family of the future preceptor of a prince.

It is still debated which of several châteaux was the birth-
place, on August 6, 1651, of François de Salignac de La Mothe-
Fénelon. The favored place is the manor later owned by "Fan-

fan," beloved great-nephew of François de Fénelon, who was the last of the family to own it. It is a fifteenth-century building with many additions, deeply scarred by fire. François was the second son of the second wife of Pons de Salignac de Fénelon, and his mother's maiden name was Louise de La Cropte de St. Arbre. There had been twelve children by his father's first marriage; there were four by his second.

It was in the year of François's birth that Louis XIV attained his majority at the age of thirteen, having been king of France since his fifth year. His tremendous reign of seventy-two years —the longest in European history—was already started on its astonishing course. The struggle of the Fronde was over and in 1651 Louis XIV was declared monarch of France. An absolute monarch he intended to be and was so in very truth—a fact which greatly modified Fénelon's later career as a churchman and his influence in affairs of state. Louis XIV, with his persistent energy and passion for kingship, his boundless pride and narrow egotism, held in his hands all of France—a France that might have appeared a carefully patched and magnificently decorated vase. It was a vase so brittle, however, that the pressure of a live root might shatter it. The watchful monarch was well aware of such threatening tendrils and ruthlessly attempted to uproot them one by one as they appeared. Nevertheless, seeds of liberty grow silently and no system, no matter how carefully conceived or meticulously operated, can be secure against the inevitable stirrings of life. The contest between the formed and the formless is common in every century, but ever more so when the mold is as rigid as it was in seventeenth-century

Direction

France. François de Fénelon was not to be exempt from the
struggle. The events that were forming the character and kingly
habits of Louis were casting a long shadow over young Fénelon.

There are few records of François's childhood. It is safe to
assume that, in the sad manner of the day, all the fifteen siblings
did not live to grow up. One half brother is known to have
become a missionary to Canada, where he died. Another is said
to have been drowned. Fénelon commented in later life: "My
young days were pleasant and unrestrained, taken up with congenial studies and intercourse with delightful friends." These
are warm memories, even allowing for the rosy afterglow often
reflected back into childhood.

Fénelon left no pen picture of his mother except such reflection as is found in his treatise on the education of girls. It is
hard to think that his insight could have been so keen and
his respect for the inherent possibilities in feminine nature so
marked if he had not known some woman who seemed to have
the qualities he extolled, and who more likely than his mother?
"A woman of poise and judgment, who punctually attends her
duties, domestic and religious, is the guiding spirit of the whole
house. She so orders it as to provide for the welfare, spiritual
and temporal, of all its inmates. Nay, man, who in public affairs
has unfettered authority, can give no real effect to his resolutions unless woman lends him her co-operation. The world is
not an abstraction, a figment of the imagination; it is an aggre-
gate of all the families composing it. Who, then, is in a better
position to supervise it than woman, than the mistress of the
house, who, besides her position of authority and her continual

presence in the house, is by nature careful, attentive to detail, industrious, engaging, and persuasive? What sweetness or charm may a man look for in life if its most intimate relationship, namely, marriage, is turned to bitterness and gall? And the children, that is to say, the world of tomorrow, how will they grow up, if their mother spoils them from their tenderest years?" These sound very like the words of a man who is thinking concretely of someone who fulfills his ideal.

There is evidence of his mother's having left three hundred livres to the sanctuary of Notre-Dame de Rocamadour, an ancient shrine visited by St. Dominic on one of the many journeys from his native Spain and immortalized by the legend that Roland left there for a long period his mighty sword Durendal. The great castle of golden stone still glows on the mountainside. Evidently there was a trend toward religion on the maternal side and probably the vocation of the boy François was partially an inheritance. His constitution was always delicate and the height and leanness of his figure were doubtless evident at an early age. The vivid and prolific chronicler, Saint-Simon, speaks of his bold, although not perfect, symmetry of feature and his piercing dark eyes.

No doubt it was in these early years that Fénelon formed those habits of frugality and refined austerity which characterized his whole life. Possibly in his early home the fare for the horde of children was meager, and necessity may have provided the original tendency in the direction of leanness.

Because of his father's position in the countryside, interesting visitors were often in the château at Sarlat and his knowledge and love of the great works of antiquity might well have sprung from discussions to which he listened around the hearth or the dining table of his early home. Among these visitors was his uncle, the Marquis de Fénelon, distinguished soldier and diplomat. The marquis belonged to the Company of the Blessed Sacrament, whose aim was the moral regeneration of the country, so there fell early on the boy's ears conversations concerning the religious affairs of the time—talk too old for his head but not for his heart.

There was also a tutor, one among the many great teachers whose gifts have come to fruition in the lives of their pupils even though their own names are lost. Certainly someone nurtured in the young Fénelon an enduring fondness for classical literature; someone initiated him into habits of intellectual discipline so that he could discover, organize, and report the content of any given subject matter. Moreover, there was a sound psychology in the boy's training, for he not only looked on learning with zest and acquired it with ease, but developed a gift for passing on knowledge in the same fashion. Later in his life, when he became instructor to a prince, he threw himself into the invention of fables and games with the spontaneity of one who saw no reason to leave wit and imagination outside the pale of learning.

As part of so large a family, François never lacked for playmates nor probably for intriguing games. The countryside was the scene of many hunting expeditions in which all the men of the village, young and old, went with what weapons they had at hand into surrounding fields and woodland to hunt wolves and wild boar. Sunday and holydays of obligation were usually the time for the hunt—after Mass had been said—in order that work in the fields should not be interrupted. However, the boy François was no huntsman; he grew tall so fast that his health was not robust. His high resourcefulness made him a good companion and a leader. Traits of a delicate imagination, such as later marked the invention of *Télémaque,* probably had lively exercise in his early days.

When the matter of a career for the not-too-vigorous younger son came up for consideration the priesthood seemed an obvious choice. Certainly it was the usual vocation for a markedly intelligent son of a noble father who had more well-placed political and social connections than he had wealth. In this case, the family also had important associations in the church.

One uncle was the bishop of Sarlat whom the young Fénelon frequently visited and who restrained him from one of his early missionary projects. Another uncle was the Marquis de Fénelon who demonstrated in his religious conduct the same preciseness and perseverance that had made him illustrious as a soldier. When de Harlai, notable for his loose conduct, became archbishop of Paris, the old soldier coupled this somber admonition with his congratulations: "There is, sir, a great difference between the day when such a nomination secures you the compliments of all France and the day of your death when you will appear before God to render him an account of your office."

This sharp reckoning with time and eternity was probably no well-thought-out address; rather, the natural speech of a

man who more than twenty-four years earlier had been set
to making the same sort of reckoning. He was a disciple of
Jean Jacques Olier, who placed heavy precepts on his followers
laying upon them such rules as this: "Consider your life as a
perpetual perishing and lift up your mind to God above all
whenever the clock strikes, saying, 'God, I adore your eternal
being. I am happy that my being should perish every moment
so that every moment it may render homage to your eternity.' "

The marquis was inspired by M. Olier to oppose the time-
honored dueling custom which was increasing among the nobility. The old soldier succeeded in recruiting a large group of
notable military men and influencing them to sign a declaration
forswearing the practice. On Pentecost, 1631, this impressive
company led by the Marquis appeared before a large congregation and kneeling before M. Olier placed in his hand the document that resulted in the pope's edict against such use of
arms. This was twenty years before François's birth but the
incident was certainly handed down to him, since feats of conscience mean no less to the performer than those of physical
bravery. Integrity of conscience was an early ideal in the
Fénelon family.

Through M. Olier the marquis was also aligned with that
other stalwart activist, Vincent de Paul. And while François
was later to have a closer contact with these two protagonists
of prayer and action, he was introduced to their principles
early in life. A sympathy of spirit existed between the austere
soldier and the slender boy. François was particularly devoted
to the marquis and gleaned from him the beginnings of those

high ideals of a search for simplicity which stayed with him throughout life. The marquis gave him the same fatherly affection that he gave his only daughter—who later married Montmorency-Laval, a name that figures frequently in the family correspondence.

Although there is no record as to whether François himself had anything to do with the choice of his career, we can assume that his opinion was given weight. For if he had wanted a more physically active life there seems to have been no reason for denying him; his was a considerate and loving family in which his opinions would have had some weight. He was particularly interested in the intellectual pursuits, which he hoped would have free rein in the church.

François was twelve when he was sent to the University of Cahors. Two years later he was transferred to the College du Plessis in Paris. A university curriculum at that time consisted primarily in a thorough grounding in the humanities. Mathematics was included and philosophical discussion of science. Logic was a major discipline; the languages were certain to include Latin, with wide acquaintance of Latin and Greek literatures; philosophy and theology held a central position. At the beginning of the seventeenth century the collegiate life of the University of Paris seemed at an end and its forty colleges stood deserted, a condition due in part to the drawn-out civil wars that marked the close of the sixteenth century. It was also due in part to the ability of the Jesuits to take advantage of the conservatism of the academic authorities in Paris and to gain almost a monopoly of both higher and lower education in provincial France, so that there existed excellent schools outside of Paris. In the last quarter of the seventeenth century, however, the colleges of Paris were again on the upswing and some of them had distinguished faculties.

In the year 1672, when Fénelon was twenty-one, he became a student at Saint-Sulpice, where he was enrolled in the Petit Séminaire, a section set apart for students whose health needed guarding. His years at Saint-Sulpice determined in part the set of his character. It was there that he developed a profound regard for truth—whether or not it accorded with his own interest —discipline of mind and body, humility of spirit, respect for properly constituted authority, along with the marked independence of thought inherent in his nature.

The director of the College of Saint-Sulpice, M. Tronson, was a profound and thoughtful man who could inspire young men to a realization of the nobility of their vocation. He possessed ecclesiastical power but by preference lived a life of unostentatious seclusion. He was well aware that in his position as superior he had accepted responsibility for training the minds and characters of priests who might later become influential in affairs of state as well as church. Perhaps his most distinguishing characteristic—one which he passed on untarnished as an ideal to Fénelon—was a certain open-mindedness, a disposition to consider the opinions of others before passing judgment. Behind M. Tronson stood the saintly figure of M. Olier, who had been appointed to the parish at Saint-Sulpice some thirty years previous when it had been one of the notoriously violent sections of Paris.

There the indefatigable Olier had found plenty of poor people, plenty of criminals, plenty of vagabonds, and unbelieving liberals. M. Vincent de Paul, who with his Little Sisters of Charity and Lazarist priests had worked in the most villainous sections of France, said he sent his missionaries to Saint-Sulpice with more reluctance than he would send them to Barbary. M. Olier loved the slums and there was no misery of soul or body for which his resourcefulness did not seek a remedy. He had a genius for finding a practical and direct approach to all wretchedness that presented itself to him. He would gather the unhoused children about him as he walked the streets of his parish, or open the doors of his own poor quarters to the hungry and irreligious men and women on all sides. There was a great simplicity in his ministry; he did not analyze the strange and unhappy conditions that went to make up his world, and he gave one answer to all—the greatness of God as revealed in Jesus and the littleness of every man without him.

His passion for reform as well as the example of his consecrated life drew around him a group of devoted young priests and lay people, all of whom he set to work in the same spirit of devotion. About the time Fénelon was born, M. Olier had succeeded in erecting a square building large enough to house a hundred students, and so began the college that long after Fénelon's residence there bore the stamp of Olier's vigorous character. During this period there was being built the Church of Saint-Sulpice, an edifice that is still a place of worship. It is classic in style and as large as Notre-Dame de Paris. Its dark façade dominates that whole quarter of the city, rising high above its small shops. Albert Schweitzer says that its organ is the finest in the world. M. Olier and Dr. Schweitzer, each with a consuming passion for humanity, are linked together by deeper ties than the fact that they have walked in a common parish.

M. Olier had no place in his community for ambitious, secular priests. He insisted that they know life and its temptations, that they recognize its evils even while they were aware of their own seclusion. The heritage of devotion that M. Olier gave to Saint-Sulpice was passed on to young priests for generations. Thirty-five years later Fénelon wrote from Cambrai: "Give me kind hearts and common sense and I will undertake to set them on the right road. I will be like a brother to them. I do not ask for polish or astonishing talent, I only desire ordinary capabilities and real devotion to God."

Studies at the seminary were theological. Fénelon had from a child been a quick and proficient student of Greek classics, an interest that did not lessen as he grew older. Classical and secular courses were taken at the Sorbonne. Students lived as a community family and none, not even those of noble families, were excused from the menial duties of the house. All were encouraged to meditate upon the life of Jesus until they could reproduce *ad seriatim* the events of his life and so to lose themselves in that life that their own fortunes or misfortunes could never absorb their attention. The ceremonials of the church were observed with exactness, and obedience was required as an exercise of humility. M. Olier aimed at Christian perfection for every man who came under his direction. This same penchant he instilled in the young priests in the Saint-Sulpice community, from which came some of the most notable directors of the period. Jean Jacques Olier had passed on to M. Tronson the same standard of training.

François de Fénelon was a favorite of M. Tronson, under whose direction he placed himself entirely and from whom he learned much in the art of spiritual directing. He offered his teacher that emotional devotion which a young man accords an older person who embodies his spiritual ideal. Their relationship he cultivated with enthusiasm. He wrote the marquis a brief note saying, "I desire passionately to be able to tell you now some part of all that passes between M. Tronson and me, but indeed, monsieur, I know not how to do so." It was a friendship that continued throughout their lifetimes. One of the principles that the teacher impressed on the young priest was the need for an unfailing and constant submission of all affairs to the will of God, not nominally so, but in absolute reality. It was a lesson Fénelon was to need in the years that were opening before him. Out of the conflict of later life he wrote to Pope Clement XI: "I congratulate myself on having had M. Tronson for my instructor in the Word of Life, and having been formed under his personal care for the ecclesiastical career. Never was any man, unless I am mistaken, superior to him for love of discipline, for skill, for prudence, piety and sagacity in discernment of character."

François de Salignac de La Mothe-Fénelon was twenty-four when he received the tonsure. It was a solemn occasion, for to become a Sulpician priest meant a total dedication of

[14]

one's self to God and a separation from the world. It was a vow that Sulpicians renewed year after year.

He remained three more years with the community at Saint-Sulpice and served as one of the parish priests. As he ministered in the parish he became skilled in the art of giving in the manner of Vincent de Paul, who laid upon his missionaries and Little Sisters of Charity a rule of gentleness. He had said, "You will find that charity is a heavy burden to carry, heavier than the bowl of soup and the full basket. But you will keep your gentleness and your smile. It is not enough to give soup and bread. This the rich can do. You are the servant of the poor, always smiling, always good-humored. They are your masters, terribly sensitive and exacting masters, you will see. Then the uglier and dirtier they will be, the more unjust and insulting, the more gentle you must be. It is for your gentleness alone that the poor will forgive you the bread you give them."

These were habits of gentleness that the young priest carried with him throughout a long life. In his *Eloge* before the French Academy, d'Alembert related the following anecdote concerning the aging Fénelon, who because of his impartial charity to opposing armies in Flanders was given a safe-conduct across the battle lines. One day he observed a peasant dejected and melancholy, whose grief was so great that he could not eat. Fénelon asked him the cause of his sorrow. "Ah, sir," the peasant said, "I had a cow, the support of my family, which I had to leave behind when the enemy came. I shall never have her like again." Under the protection of his safe-conduct the venerable archbishop set off with one servant, and returned with the cow. "Unhappy those," remarked the narrator to the aristocracy of the French Academy of Letters, "to whom this affecting anecdote seems unworthy of being told before this respectable assembly."

When he left Saint-Sulpice, Fénelon had attained his full stature and bore a youthful resemblance to that personality which Saint-Simon presents as François de Fénelon, archbishop of Cambrai: "He was a tall, thin man, well made, with a large nose, eyes whence fire and wit issued like a torrent and a countenance such as I have never seen in any other person, and which though seen but once, could never be forgotten. It combined everything, yet its contrasts did not conflict. It possessed gravity and courtesy; solemnity and gaiety; it was equally expressive of the learned man, the bishop and aristocrat; but what dominated his face, as indeed his whole person, was thought, intellect, grace, propriety, and above all nobility. One had to make an effort to cease looking at him. There was, too, a sympathetic merging of his own personality with that of the friend with whom he was speaking, a subtle and inborn grace which made some say, 'his friends love him because they see themselves in him.'"

The evaluation of the seventeenth-century priest is echoed by Francis Thompson in his *Literary Criticisms* as he speaks of the feminine quality in Fénelon's character: ". . . those moods and subtleties, all these things were feminine, so was his unaccountability to himself. He was exactly the character to arouse warring judgments. Quick, mobile, intelligent, various, of sympathetic adaptability, a man of many characters, yet far from a man of no character; this heterogeneity always fares ill at the hands of an impatient world, which loves to clap a hasty label on its great men and know they are ready docketed for future use. It was his tongue, like Johnson's, which gave him the greatest influence in his lifetime."

Perhaps this was the simplicity to which Fénelon aspired in that long letter to his friend which describes the meaning of simplicity—"the rightness of things," as he says. Such simplicity he indicates is puzzling, "seems a little careless and more irregular, but it has a feeling of frankness and truth which makes us conscious of a certain openness, gentleness, innocence, gaiety, and serenity, which is charming when we see it near to and continually with pure eyes." He learned early to assume various characters without change of his essential spirit.

2

The Beginning Way

IT WAS during the period of his priesthood at Saint-Sulpice that Fénelon began to dream of becoming a foreign missionary. Like other enthusiasts of his day, his ardor for saving souls was colored by genuine appreciation of strange cultures and recently-discovered lands, and by literary enthusiasm which enhanced rather than detracted from his evangelizing zeal. Canada was denied him because of his lack of robustness, and his thoughts turned to the Near East. Even at this early age he aspired to unify the secular and the religious in his daily life. All in one paragraph he proposed to proclaim "the advent of an Unknown God . . . to cull the laurels of Delphi . . . revel in the delights of Tempe." Never for him were politics, social relationships, and religion walled off one from another.

In 1679 he went to Sarlat to visit his uncle, the bishop, and before returning wrote to Jacques Bénigne Bossuet, his warm friend and bishop of Condom in Gascony:

The Beginning Way

A number of little things have been occurring, one after another, to delay my return to Paris; but at last, monseigneur, I am starting. I feel almost as if I could fly. With this journey in front of me my thoughts have been dwelling on one longer still. The whole of Greece lies open before me. The Sultan shrinks back in terror. Already the Peloponnesus is breathing the air of freedom, and the Church of Corinth is about to put forth new bloom. The voice of the Apostle shall again be heard in the land. I feel as though I had again been wafted on wings of those noble scenes and priceless ruins, there to refresh my soul, not only with the sight of those wondrous buildings, but to bathe it in the very spirit of antiquity. I turn my steps toward the Areopagus where, to the sages of the world, St. Paul proclaimed the advent of the Unknown God. But after the sacred comes the profane, and I do not forget to make my way down to Piraeus, where Socrates is busily engaged planning the scene of his ideal Republic. I scale the twin peaks of Parnassus and cull the laurels of Delphi; I revel in the delights of Tempe. When shall the blood of the Turks mingle with the blood of the Persians on the plains of Marathon, so that the whole of Greece may be given up to religion, philosophy, and the fine arts, which look upon her as their native home?

I shall not forget thee, O Isle made sacred by the heavenly visions of the beloved disciple! O happy Patmos, I shall go and, on thy soil kiss the very ground whereon the apostle trod, and I shall seem to behold the heavens opening above me. My bosom shall swell with indignation against the false prophet who was fain to take it upon himself to unfold the oracles of the true one, and I shall bless the Almighty for that He, far from casting down the Church in a fall like Babylon's flung chains about the dragon and gave her the victory. Already I see the end of the Great Schism and the reuniting of East and West. Asia I behold, the sound of her sighs reaching even to the banks of the Euphrates, seeing the day dawn again, when the long night is past: the land hallowed by the Savior's steps and watered with his blood, set free from its desecrators and clothed in fresh glory; lastly the children of Abraham, scattered over the face of the earth, more numerous than the stars in heaven, who, gathered together from the four corners of the world, shall come in their hosts to acknowledge the Christ whom they pierced. But enough, monseigneur; I will desist. You will be relieved to hear that this is my last letter and my final outburst of enthusiasm, for you may be finding it rather importunate. Pray, excuse it as eloquent of my longing to converse with you from afar, ere yet I can do so face to face.

This is the letter of a young man, in whom love of literature and learning is both inborn and cultivated, to whom the unseen is more real than the seen and the cause greater than any of its adherents. There is humor in the letter; the enthusiastic writer appraises his own enthusiasm. He enjoys indulging his eloquence and sharing his panegyrics with a sympathetic older friend. There is every reason to believe that Fénelon would gladly have gone to the far corners of the earth with zeal for his missions had he been permitted to do so.

His call came from another direction. At the suggestion of Jacques Bénigne Bossuet, the king appointed the young priest as principal of the Nouvelles Catholiques. This was a community founded by the archbishop of Gondi in 1634 for the purpose of instructing young women interested in or newly converted to Catholicism. The king had a great interest in this institution and included it among many such projects for the conversion of Protestants—an activity that amounted almost to a passion as he advanced in years. Fénelon's zeal, intelligence, and singleness of purpose had made its mark on churchmen who were looking for able young priests. He accepted his post and brought to it the zest that distinguished him in whatever work he undertook. The new charge, however, did not appeal to his ideals of service as had the challenge of missionary labor with its privation and danger, but it was an avenue to a life that was to make demands no less real upon them.

Now, at twenty-seven, he went to live with his uncle, the marquis, at his apartment in the Abbey de Saint-Germain-des-Prés, within the great gray walls that saw so much of the history of the ancient Lutetia. This church with its adjacent abbey was the most ancient in Paris. It was on the Left Bank, where Dante as a student stalked down the Rue du Fouarre. Happily the church still stands, one of the most impressive edifices of the city, with its great gray walls and dignified Romanesque nave and transept. Gone are the fruit trees that bloomed against the bleak stone during the Middle Ages.

In his uncle's household Fénelon spent ten of the most tranquil and happy years of his life. It was a period of expanding powers and of realizing potentialities. Saint-Sulpice was near at hand, so M. Tronson continued as his spiritual preceptor, yet the young abbé was far enough removed from the narrow walls of the community to allow for expansion of his intellectual powers in a widening circle of cultured and earnest friends. The urbane and religiously intentioned group that had gathered around the marquis accepted him almost immediately. Indeed, his natural grace and sensitivity, his personal habits of simplicity and gentleness, combined with a quick intelligence and youthful reticence, attracted to him men and women of high spiritual quality. Among these were several families favorably received by the king. His closest friends were the Ducs de Beauvilliers and de Chévreuse, and their wives, daughters of Colbert, former minister of finance, and Jacques Bénigne Bossuet, bishop of Meaux since 1681.

Although Fénelon seems never to have striven for preferment, much less friendship, his popularity in noble circles could well be looked upon as personal ambition. The society of Louis XIV's day was a wide avenue by which an ambitious young abbé could approach the court and eventually become a cardinal or other high dignitary. The Fénelon of that period was very different from the mellow figure of the latter years. There was perhaps a tinge of youthful self-consciousness and even arrogance in the sureness with which he spoke of the spiritual life. A fervent and devoted priest, he was always; nevertheless, there is a cleverness in the very early letters and a subtleness of mind that was tempered by the fires of adversity into the serene light that illumined the archbishop of Cambrai and by which he is most commonly viewed by his admirers. If he had not been ambitious at this stage of his growth he would have been unnatural. The very fact that he has been called both too ambitious and too retiring by his contemporaries, notably by Saint-Simon and de Harlai, tends to show that he was neither in excess; and who can expect the mellowness of sunset light to illumine the feverish summits and depressions of youth's landscapes? No doubt both ambition and modesty were facets of the young priest's personality and he presented to himself as well as to others all the complexities of a young man trying to find his true place in the world.

It is necessary to know Jacques Bénigne Bossuet in order to have an understanding of Fénelon's relations to the ecclesiastical turmoil that marked the period, for no other individual had so much to do with his fate and fortunes. Bossuet, a native of Dijon, appeared outwardly serene, placid, and hearty; a massive Burgundian typifying common-sense and middle-class conservatism. By 1680 he had achieved not only his position as the most eloquent preacher in Paris, but was also the Gallican church's most ardent advocate. His genius surging from the pulpit of the Royal Chapel had a way of igniting dry logic with such passion as to start fires burning in the hearts of his hearers. His accusation that Luther could "fling his fury into theses" applied equally well to himself. He was a veteran of many ecclesiastical combats with the Calvinists. Two of his masterful funeral sermons, probably second to none of their kind, were delivered at about this time; one at the funeral of Henrietta Maria, widow of Charles I, the other at the funeral of her daughter, Henrietta, Duchess of Orleans. The former contains passages still moving to the modern reader. As tutor to the dauphin his great treatises on the nature of God and man, the history of God's dealings with men and the code of man's rights and duties based on these dealings, thundered forth to the court of Louis XIV. Bossuet was a hard-working, conscientious scholar; indeed, in his school days his fellow students had nicknamed him *Bos suetus aratro*—an ox broken to the plow. Although he was Fénelon's senior by twenty-four years, strength spoke to strength between the two men. Their early friendship was built on a foundation of mutual respect. With both, devotion to their church was stronger than any other attachment.

Baron Friedrich von Hugel has described Bossuet as hard and

sensible, and Fénelon as elastic and exquisite. In the light of their similar and dissimilar characteristics and of the contrasting vicissitudes of their environment, it seems inevitable that these two strong personalities should be either great friends or great enemies as their changing personalities and the march of events directed. They could not be indifferent to each other.

Fénelon was an aristocrat by birth, his nobility extending back five centuries; Bossuet's grandfather had been a draper and his father a small lawyer. In seventeenth-century France the gap between the two families was more significant than it would be today and even more so than it would have been just before the Revolution. Both men aspired to ecclesiastical office. Fénelon, by natural ability and noble birth, was in line for advancement regardless of scholarship. Bossuet, who also possessed natural ability for the church, was required to work ten years for his doctor's degree before he could qualify for an episcopate. Both men possessed high integrity in regard to the priesthood; both had imbibed the ideals of Olier and Vincent de Paul—Bossuet directly and Fénelon through Tronson at Saint-Sulpice. About each of them revolved a group of men and women seeking spiritual counsel. Fénelon was always able to find a point of contact with those about him, enjoying the interplay of mind with mind while Bossuet soon outstripped those about him and led them where he himself wanted to go. Fénelon's quick intelligence and natural imagination colored his conversation, making it sparkle with apt anecdote and bright repartee, while Bossuet's prosaic and scholarly temperament kept him to the somber and solid consideration of a serious subject. Both were impassioned and brilliant preachers: Fénelon warm and earnest, Bossuet theological and fiery; Fénelon speculative and mystical; Bossuet logical and stern. Both had an ideal of perfection but they were idealists at different stages and with different means. Fénelon was a contemplative, Bossuet was an ascetic. Bossuet was fifty-two and Fénelon was twenty-eight; one was a hardened tree, the other had not lost his suppleness.

As one may appreciate more easily the fluid grace of the stream against the immovable banks, just so against the steadfast Bossuet the litheness of Fénelon's spirit is revealed. Bossuet accepted the harsh ethics of Port-Royal, he found spiritual strength in the asceticism of la Trappe. External order, implacable rule, and immutable uniformity characterized his means to perfection. In Fénelon there is a happier harmony between body and spirit. He did not say the self was detestable; rather, that there was an appropriateness of being for all creatures, and one loved himself in the light of such relevancy as he did his neighbor; he would temper religious exercise to the strength of the body; he would enlarge the heart to recognize God in the beauty of nature and art; for him spontaneity, impulse and liberty were the fruits of holy living. "Everything breathes in him that fullness and happy harmony of life," says Henri Martin, "which the poets of the Middle Ages expressed by the beautiful word *liesse,* gladness, and which they did not separate from valor and virtue."

These two strong personalities offer together "the eternal duality of strength and grace; one is Michelangelo, but a

Michelangelo more serene and more antique—and the other is Raphael; one is Corneille, and the other is Racine. . . . One overawes, the other softens; one inspires fear of God, the other trust in God," continues the historian Martin.

At this particular phase of their lives they needed each other. Bossuet's assurance, combined with his forthright extraversion, furnished a kind of strength and security to the tall, lean young priest whose mind moved more tentatively, always seeking two or more sides of a question, experimenting in life with the principles and theories learned in seminary days. Also to the matter-of-fact, pessimistic Bossuet there was no doubt charm in the younger man's erudition, which was unembarrassed by a playful and poetic cast of thought.

During the years Bossuet was so constantly employed at court as tutor of the dauphin he frequently retired to his country place, Germigny, a solitude that he treasured exceedingly. Only near friends were ever permitted to visit this retreat—among them was Fénelon, and early in their friendship they spent much time together in its quiet surroundings. Bossuet was an encyclopedia of information on philosophy, theology, and history. After the intellectual narrowness of Saint-Sulpice and the often superficial conversations of court life, Germigny offered a happy haven for them both. Deep and intimate religious searching occupied them, however, on occasion, as later correspondence reveals. A warm affection grew between them, as is shown in a whimsical letter from Fénelon after he left Paris for Saintonge: "If they keep us much longer away from you we will suppress the *Ave* or perhaps tumble into some monstrous heresy, in order to ensure a lucky disgrace that may take us back to Germigny."

While Bossuet was still at court his daily walks in the park at Versailles became a sort of educational institution for the young intellectuals who gathered around him to exchange their thoughts on poetry, art, and religion or to criticize one another's manuscripts. It became known as the Allée des Philosophes, and the little group that assembled there was called the Little Council. Among those who participated in these daily discussions were Fénelon, the Abbé de Langeron, Fénelon's nephew and lifelong friend, and the Abbé Fleury. In time Bossuet led them to an assiduous study of the Scriptures, into which all plunged with youthful zeal. It was at this period that the famous Richard Simon and Père Dupin were arousing churchmen with their critical histories and translations of the Old and New Testaments. The sturdy figure of the Burgundian could be seen day after day expounding to the young priests the true faith while the Abbé Fleury, with his pen in one hand and his Bible in the other, meticulously set down in its margins the commentary for the day. These sessions expanded until they came to be held regularly in the rooms of their leader, who after a frugal supper gave his best powers to shaping a suitable and orthodox commentary. The Abbé de Langeron commented that the fare supplied to the body at Bossuet's table was by no means so good as the mental fare that followed.

Through the influence of Bossuet in 1685, Fénelon was appointed to direct a group of priests in an effort to convert the Protestants at Saintonge to Catholicism. His success at the Nouvelles Catholiques merited him attention, but it is doubtful that this sort of assignment would have come by his own choice because his was not a nature given to the use of force, let alone to persecution. It may well have been that his superiors felt that his reputation for fair-mindedness and his nobility of spirit might register on the right side of the ledger of public opinion regarding the treatment of Protestants at a time when there was so much restiveness as a result of the peremptory Revocation that deprived them of freedom to worship.

The struggle of the church to stamp out the Huguenots had been a continuing war for nearly a century, marked by decades of horrible fighting and persecution. The Massacre of St. Bartholomew in 1572 and consequent persecution had resulted in solidifying the Protestant forces and giving them strength enough to win the Edict of Nantes in 1598. This act, assuring them liberty of conscience throughout France, was more or less in force until 1685 when the impact of the Catholic forces against it made it impossible to enforce. It became one of those laws which were on the books, but it was flagrantly disobeyed and disregarded because they ran counter to the king's policy. Louis XIV with his growing religious interest felt that his own salvation was dependent upon the conversion of the Huguenots. He was convinced that by the salvation of heretics his own sins, and they were many, could be atoned for. Therefore, after the Revocation he bent all his powers to enroll them in the church. At the time he declared that he would complete the conversion of the heretics "even if it cost him his right hand." History has proved that the act did not strengthen the church; instead, it instituted the anticlerical movement of the century and accomplished the evil consequence that the king himself had predicted.

It would be comforting to report that Fénelon refused to countenance the quartering of troops in recalcitrant households, that he would have no traffic with those who urged men against their consciences, that he appealed to the king for further consideration of the Edict. Such steps are possible in a democracy. But the situation is different with minds conditioned to an absolute monarchy, even though by nature they are revolutionary minds. The authority of the king was taken for granted; a priest is trained to absolute obedience to the church. Then, too, Fénelon may have had secret hopes of converting the Protestants under his jurisdiction by milder methods than terror and bribery. Here was a curious predicament for a man who loved peace, justice, and reasonableness as did Fénelon.

He went a long way in the direction of justice in refusing to admit the dragoons into partnership with the work of the church and in insisting that they be withdrawn from all places under his jurisdiction. He knew as well as any other the terrorizing tactics they used as common weapons against all heretics. When the persecution was at its height many priests followed the king's lead in feeling that forcible conversion was better than none at all; they walked straight into the chambers of the dying, ordered heretic relatives from the room and threatened the sick man with the flames of hell. Fénelon followed a more sensible and humane policy. When called by a Catholic relative of a dying heretic, he used a prayer that he had composed especially for such last-hour conversions, a prayer which concluded with the words, "Thou knowest, my Savior, that I desire to live and die in the Truth, forgive me if I was mistaken." Such gentleness toward sinners was a most unusual pattern for either Catholic or Protestant to follow in days when antipathy between sects was exceedingly violent.

Something of his reasonableness must have won him a hearing. After six months in Saintonge, he wrote unofficially to a friend: "It would be easy enough to prevail on our sailors in their present condition to confess and communicate if—for the glory of our mission—we chose to do so." He had, however, too high a regard for the privilege of becoming a part of the church to press for unwilling recipients of salvation. "Of what avail is confession to those who do not acknowledge the true church, nor her power to forgive sin?" Years later, replying to a question from M. de Noailles, he made a thoughtful observation based on his work in Saintonge: "It does not seem to me desirable to torment foreign heretic soldiers with efforts to convert them; it does not succeed; it forces them into hypocrisy instead, and they desert in shoals. It is enough to forbid them the exercise of their religion as the king desires."

If he had spiritual counsel from any of his friends in the direction of fair-mindedness, it is not recorded. Certainly Mme. de Maintenon, one of Fénelon's recently acquired friends, evinced nothing but complacent sympathy with repressive measures. She was always an influence on the side of intolerance and severity toward the Protestants, whispering encouragement toward further harshness in the ears of Louis XIV whenever he showed signs of relenting. The mid-seventeenth century was a cruel age when the immense privileges of the aristocracy and, in a lesser sense, those of the rising class of bourgeois financial magnates cast into deep shadow the lives of over-burdened peasants and other humble workers. It was only one hundred years until the fall of the Bastille, and although the break in the dike was hardly yet an actual fact, still an observant watcher could perceive—and some, including Fénelon, were beginning to do so—a thin fissure forming, spreading, and threatening to undermine the whole top-heavy edifice of the French social structure.

It is quite possible, of course, that Fénelon may have registered protests with those higher in authority but that his protests were ignored; the obscurity of the novice missionary at this time make it unlikely that any such documents would have been preserved.

In Saintonge, as in Paris, he was a preacher who spoke from the heart as well as from the head, and such a message answered the needs of men and women around him. On December 28, 1685, he wrote to Mme. de Beauvilliers: "The whole people here are beginning to love us; crowds run to hear our instructions; they stop us in the street to talk to us. 'They are good people,' they say, speaking of us, 'they preach the gospel well.' You would be pleased to see us embracing these shopkeepers and sailors. The praise they give us is useful to them and does us no harm; it is useful to make them docile and the roughness of these people here is a good preservative against the temptations of vainglory, when they praise us." In the light of Fénelon's lifelong attitude these are not words of conscious superiority so much as objective reporting.

All was not going easily for him. Three weeks later he wrote again to the duchess: "I beg you to have M. the Marquis de Seigneley read this secretly: we have found in the spirits of all here *an unbelievable attachment to heresy*; nevertheless, they seem to be struck by our instructions so that they even burst into tears, but the cabal among them, and the poisonous letters which they receive from their ministers, who have gone to Holland, soon upset all these good beginnings."

The current attitude toward skeptics and unbelievers was much more tolerant than toward Protestants. Atheists got off scot-free; men who went to no church at all could go and come as they liked without molestation. To many Catholics as well as Protestants there seemed irony in letting agnostics die in peace, sinners though they were and destined to damnation, while those who were Protestants for conscience' sake were hounded by both civil and ecclesiastical authorities. From the Catholic point of view the agnostic at worst was only a passive influence while the Protestant was deliberately instigating a schism, breaking apart the body of Christ, tearing the branches from the true Vine. Also from the standpoint of the state the dissident Protestants were a greater danger to the stability of government. Fénelon himself felt that the civil power had a right to maintain or to re-establish religious unity. His objection to force at this point was on the grounds not of its illogicality but of its uselessness. As a patriot he was sometimes alarmed. After he had been on his mission for more than a year he wrote: "Our arrival in this country, joined to the rumors of war that come ceaselessly from Holland, make these people believe that they are feared and that we are handling them with gloves. They convince themselves that some great revolution will soon occur, and that the powerful army of the Dutch is fated to come to deliver them . . . The pastoral letters of Jurieu and the numberless other letters from Holland are upsetting everybody's brains . . . As soon as one seems to spare them, they conclude that the king is forced to it by the state of foreign affairs . . . It is less important to the king to fortify the frontiers than to make safe this open coastline, where there are numberless heretics, who, by a forced abjuration, have only become more bitter against the church and against the king; and from them may be expected the most extreme violence should there come troubled times." His appraisal was reasonable enough, for the Huguenots did continue to make trouble for the state and to draw down the ire of neighboring Protestant nations upon the French government; an antagonism which did not matter too much while Louis XIV was in his heyday but which later worked no good for France.

Years later, when Fénelon preached his sermon *Pour le Sacre de l'Electeur de Cologne*, he referred to his experience at Saintonge. "Can force persuade men? Can it make them do what they do not wish to do? Is it not evident that the most humble of men of the people do not always believe or wish according to the taste of the most powerful princes? Everyone is silent, everyone is unhappy, everyone disguises his feelings . . . everyone flatters, everyone applauds; but no one believes and no one loves in the least; on the contrary, everyone hates the more that he patiently endures the constraint that reduces him to pretend to love. No human power can force the impenetrable suppression of the heart's liberty . . . Coercion makes the last remnants of pride revolt; it leaves in the heart a wound which very easily becomes infected." Here is the lesson of Saintonge—and one well worth the long months of labor and loneliness that Fénelon put into his mission: "No human power can force the impenetrable suppression of the heart's liberty."

Fénelon returned happily to his work with the Nouvelles Catholiques, took up his quarters again in the Abbey de Saint-Germain-des-Prés, and joined his old friends. It proved to be his last period of relative retirement and one in which he was most free from public responsibility. Socially he was more sought after than before and more in demand as a spiritual director. His experience at Saintonge had deepened his own religious life and consequently his understanding of others. He was regarded as a person of high integrity and one who was capable of achieving his ideal. He had leisure to write and a growing confidence in his pen. This gained for him a place in the French Academy by 1693.

There was prevalent in the court at this time an interest in personal spiritual growth and priests were being called upon to exercise the fine art of counseling the nobility. Among these men and women there were many sincere seekers, while others were merely bored with the emptiness of luxurious living, and religion became for them a faddish sort of introspection and diversion. Some priests were particularly skillful in the psychological assistance they were able to offer these anxious persons, while others were unscrupulous. The evils of such a wave of self-concern are implicit. The director became the butt of all the trivial misdemeanors and morbid self-analysis in which bored and idle women were likely to engage and in doing so acquired power to achieve his own selfish ends. La Bruyère commented on this fashion of having a spiritual director: "What sort is the lady who has a director? Is she kinder to her husband and gentler to her servants? Is she one with a less execrable temper, and a lesser relish for the comforts of life? No, not a bit of it. What, then, is she? Just a lady who has a director."

Fénelon early became an expert in these matters and had both patience with the sincere seeker and a forthrightness with the insincere that challenged them to greater endeavor or dissuaded them from further trifling. Schooled in the ways of St. François de Sales, he was gentle but none the less honest with every soul who depended on him for direction. At this time he wrote to Mme. de Maintenon:

"That I of which I have so often spoken to you is still with you—an idol which you have not yet broken. You wish to go to God with your whole heart, but not by the loss of the *I*; on the contrary, you seek the *I* in God."

Mme. de Maintenon was one of the intimates of a very small

circle that met weekly to discuss the spiritual life at the Hôtel de Beauvilliers. The Duchesse de Beauvilliers and her sister, the Duchesse de Chévreuse, with their husbands constituted this little group that welcomed the young Fénelon on his return from Saintonge. Mme. de Maintenon was to figure largely in the development of Fénelon's career. She was a woman of great strength and great weakness—although she possessed a strong will she was never able to unify her ambitions. She longed for great spirituality even while she struggled to attain a place of honor with the king. Her biographers use similar phrases to describe her: very charming, dignified in manner, demure, self-restrained, cold in temperament, loving sobriety and reason in thought and action; sincerely if not passionately religious, faithful in responsibility. At this very time Fénelon described her character in a letter he wrote in response to one of hers requesting an examen. It has pamphletlike proportions. In part it reads:

"I will tell you what I think and God will help you make what use of it you please. . . . You are candid and natural; hence it comes about that you behave very kindly, without having any occasion to think about it, to those for whom you have appreciation and esteem, but you are too cold where you do not feel this appreciation. And when you are cold your coldness goes very far. I imagine in your character there is hastiness and deliberation at the same time. That which wounds you wounds you very deeply.

"You have naturally a great sense of honor, that is to say, of that honor which the world esteems and considers proper pride, but which in reality is all the more evil because we are not ashamed to call it good; we should correct ourselves more easily of a foolish vanity. You have still a great deal of this vainglory without being conscious of it. Your extreme sensitiveness about things which can wound it to the quick proves that it is certainly not extinct. You think very much still of the esteem of good people and of their approbation, you feel a conscious satisfaction in bearing your prosperity with moderation, and finally, you like others to see that your heart is superior even to your exalted position. . . . You are naturally kind and inclined to give your confidence, perhaps even too readily, to good people whose prudence you have not sufficiently sounded. But when you begin to distrust . . . It is believed in the world that you love what is good with a sincere love. Many people thought for a long time that it was only the desire for your own honor which made you take this part; but it seems to me that they understand the thing better now, and they give you credit for the purity of your motives. They still say, however, and apparently with truth, that you are cold and severe, and that with you no one must have any faults; and that, being hard to yourself, you are hard also to others; that when you begin to find any weakness in the persons from whom you expected perfection you are disgusted with them too suddenly, and you carry your disgust too far. . . . It is said that you interfere too much with affairs of state. . . . As for you, madame, it is not well for you to make efforts to remedy that which is not in your hands. Your zeal for the salvation of the king should not make you go beyond the bounds which Providence seems to have marked out for you. You must wait for the time which God alone knows, and which is in His power alone. . . ."

At this period Mme. de Maintenon was governess of the king's children by his current mistress, Mme. de Montespan, and also the king's unofficial confidante and adviser—an extremely delicate position. Her father had been imprisoned as a Huguenot malcontent and the child herself was born in prison. Her mother had her christened a Catholic, but later a relative converted her to Protestantism. The state entered in and removed her to Catholic guardianship and she was reconverted to the church. She and her mother remained penniless until 1652, when the girl married Scarron, the famous poet and satirist. For eight years there gathered in their home the most famous and brilliant men and women of all France. Scarron died in 1660 and Anne of Austria continued her pension so that she was able to maintain the same social prominence. Although society at this time of Louis XIV's reign was particularly frivolous and extravagant, a current of religious thought was creeping in. Bossuet was beginning to preach in Paris. Mme. Scarron was attracted to his sermons, and although she adhered to the external regulations and directed her actions by the advice of her confessor, the Abbé Gobelin, a severe Jesuit, she depended on Bossuet as a personal teacher and it was Bossuet who later persuaded her that she was to be the instrument of the king's conversion.

Mme. de Montespan, the king's vicious although brilliant mistress, was attracted to this vigorous and well-educated woman who was known for her dependable character and re-sourcefulness. She persuaded the king to put her in charge of their illegitimate children. Mme. Scarron was thrifty in addition to her other qualities and acquired the Maintenon estate. When the king decided to bring his children to court he also brought their governess. Here she played an extraordinarily difficult role with skill. From her position as servant to the king's mistress she advanced steadily to such influence with him that she was made a marquise. Either because she resented the superior, although unofficial rank of Mme. de Montespan or because she honestly believed the king's spasmodic attempts at morality were genuine, she was instrumental in effecting a reconciliation with the queen for a time and the latter was reinstated. The queen died in 1683 and in 1685 Mme. de Maintenon was married to Louis XIV, although she was never made queen. It was in this period just before her marriage that she came under the influence of Fénelon's fine mind and stalwart integrity.

The other members of the little group were the most idealistic and thoroughly Christian of any of those attached to the court. They held high rank among the nobles and had made their weight felt during the time when Mme. de Montespan was in power. They refused to recognize her or any other of the king's mistresses. This attitude had naturally endeared them to Mme. de Maintenon so that when she came to power she welcomed them as intimate friends. In the little gatherings at the Hôtel de Beauvilliers there was an ease in relationships and a release for all from the boring formalities of court life. The

Duc de Beauvilliers was one of the most distinguished of the courtiers and the most unaffected by his surroundings. Saint-Simon, who was his warm admirer, set him down as "one indifferent to places and cabals and worldly advantages, content when called to the Council Board simply to state his true opinion without much caring whether it was followed or not, but sitting there like a monk, who should be exemplary in his attendance at the offices, yet thinking it enough to repeat the Psalms in their accustomed rhythm, bringing little of his heart or his attention to bear thereon."

Christopher Sower, a Philadelphia Quaker of 1750, describes him in the preface to *A Treatise on Pure Love*, as one possessing all those sober virtues coveted by weighty Friends; he was modest, sedate, disinterested, liberal, sincere, polite, regular in everything, "and all of these received a luster and perfection from an eminent piety." His was not an interesting personality, but good and loyal. His friendship for Fénelon never wavered throughout the twenty-five years they were associated—seventeen years of this time they were separated by the distance of Cambrai from Versailles, a distance neither of them was permitted to span.

In contrast to the solemn primness and reserve of the Duc de Beauvilliers was set the erratic and enthusiastic Duc de Chévreuse, his brother-in-law and close confidant. Saint-Simon remarks: "They had but one set of thoughts between them." This lifelong friend may also be seen against the mirror of one of Fénelon's letters written in reply to one in which gout and Jansenism, educational theory and mortgages had jostled with his current state of soul. His spiritual adviser sorted out all his concerns one by one and then suggested how he might handle the multiplicity of affairs: "I have often noticed that you were always in a hurry to go from one occupation to another while at the same time each particular thing carries you too far. This is because you give way overmuch to your tendency to dissect everything. You are not slow, but you are lengthy. You spend a great deal of time upon each thing, not from slowness of action—on the contrary, your work is often hurried—but owing to the quantity of detail that you take in. You want to say everything that has even the smallest connection with what is in hand, you are always afraid of not saying enough; and this makes every proceeding too long and obliges you constantly to hurry from one thing to another without interval." And again he writes: "Sobriety is what you need, sobriety of thought and language, and that is only to be gained by prayer; you should proclaim a solemn fast from argument and cut things short from morn to night."

It was through his association with this little group that Fénelon would secure his next post. When de Beauvilliers was made governor of the king's grandson, he suggested that the young Abbé de Fénelon be appointed preceptor. Mme. de Maintenon added the weight of her influence to the nomination. Just prior to this appointment he had written his *Treatise on the Education of Girls*, a document that had been popularly well received. His two friends, the Abbé de Langeron and the Abbé Fleury also were appointed to the household of the Duke of Burgundy. These were the friends who in a way were to map the temporal course of his life but he, on the other hand, was to direct their spirits to a more spiritual course.

3

Early Writings

THROUGHOUT a varied career Fénelon held posts of authority, some of them requiring considerable administrative capacity and all of them constant application of mental and physical energy. Indeed, application of spiritual energy also, if the particular combination of insight and longing that calls for men's best for the sake of their own souls can be given a name apart. But he was never merely a man of action, a relatively easy category to fill no matter how demanding a task may be. He was also a priest given to contemplation; his mind delighted in analysis of cause and effect; he felt his way among the motivations that inspire action, and never lost sight of the human element even when delving into the intricacies of theology. Moreover, like most clerics of the time, he liked to set his conclusions down on paper. Perhaps the writing helped him to define his thought; perhaps he knew that his imagination leashed to a pen could more safely be depended upon not to fly off into the daydreams that have been the despair of many a monk on his knees; perhaps his unknown tutor had taught him to realize his gift for writing. Then, too, written discourse was expected of a man of his attainments. Whatever the reason for his writing, the result was noteworthy. Among the thousands of pages that must have come from his pen are many paragraphs worth spiritual pondering today and many more that are interesting because they reflect the needs, passions, and aspirations of his own day.

One of the first of his written treatises to attract wide attention was the discourse on the education of girls which he produced at the request of his warm friend and patroness, Mme. de Beauvilliers. The entire document, *Traité de l'Education des Filles*, is filled with common sense, surprising for its time and interesting at any time. Being himself a bachelor, he maintained a perspective concerning domestic life. But having grown up in a large family he also knew the ways of adolescent girls. In the days of his work among the children of the poor he had learned about the foibles of the young.

He made no attempt to analyze the personalities of the eight daughters, but instead offered sound and daring advice of a general nature. According to Macaulay, the lady of the manor of that day was acquainted with two books: a prayer book and a book of recipes. "If a damsel had the least smattering of literature, she was regarded as a prodigy." Ladies highly born and bred were expected to misspell their words and to be innocent of punctuation. Fénelon thought more highly of the female intellect and certainly brought some discernment to bear upon the influence of women on the structure and quality of society.

His essay opens with a strong assertion: "Nothing is more neglected than girls' education. . . . Look at the boys, on the other hand. For them no trouble, no expense, is spared. Look at the money spent on their books and the instruments for scientific research; look at the trouble that is taken to teach them foreign languages and such matters. As for girls, they are taught nothing, lest they be taught too much. It is currently held that an influence in things intellectual makes them vain and affected. It is quite enough for them to learn to manage a house and obey their husbands. The supporters of this theory are not slow in quoting examples to show what a ridiculous creature book learning will make of a woman." He admits that no one wants to make a bluestocking of a girl, but feels that these pointless arguments are no reason to have girls brought up by mothers who are both ignorant and thoughtless; there is a golden mean. "Women, as a rule, have less intellectual stamina and more inquisitiveness than men." Therefore, he feels, it would be inappropriate for them to study too deeply. "They don't have to rule the country, go to the wars, or become priests." Why, then, should they study politics, jurisprudence, philosophy, and theology? "Mechanical arts are unsuited to their physique; neither their bodies nor their minds are as strong, as robust as man's. On the other hand, Nature has made them industrious, and endowed them with a taste for orderliness and household management, so as to keep them quietly and comfortably at home."

The mere fact that he was discussing the education of girls was enough to shock many; his views—often conservative in retrospect—were ultraliberal for his time, and he knew it. It is a reflection on the attitude of the seventeenth century that he could say, "But if women are naturally the weaker vessels, what then? The weaker they are, the more important it is to strengthen them." However, he does go on to build up their importance. "Have they not duties to fulfill, duties which are the basis of all human life? Is it not they who make or mar the happiness of their households, who regulate every detail of family life and who, therefore, have control of everything which most intimately concerns the human race? From which it follows that they are the determining factors in the good or evil behavior of the whole world.

"A woman's occupations are hardly less important to the common weal than a man's. . . . Virtue is as essential in a woman as in a man—men think more so—and apart from the good or evil they can do in the world, they form one half of the human race redeemed by the Blood of Jesus Christ and destined to eternal life." He then points out that the ill-training of a mother results not only in poorly trained daughters but in defective male education, and mentions the part women have played in instigating wars and revolutions—no doubt alluding particularly to the women who conspired in the war of the Fronde.

In a later section he discusses the kind of education necessary.

Training should start early; the passions are present in infancy. "The brain of a child is moist and tender, the impressions it receives are deep as well as lasting"; the vivid images of the elderly are the result of these early impressions; convictions established in the very young are usually there to stay. The quick impressions of children have to be augmented by reason, developed through discipline and patience. A child's mental processes, he says, are like a candle burning in a draft, never steady; therefore the blasts of reason must not be too strong. "Answer what he asks you, freely; let him ply you with questions to the top of his bent; encourage and sustain his curiosity; enrich his memory with a fund of good material."

One especially modern point was stressed: learning must never be made synonymous with constraint, boredom, or severity; lessons must be made pleasurable and attractive. The joy of acquiring knowledge and not the hope of some extraneous reward should motivate young pupils; teachers should be agreeable, both in their physical make-up and in their personalities. But for all his emphasis on means and ends, Fénelon steered clear of setting up an educational system; his was the theory of fitting the glove to the hand, remembering, however, what duties a hand has to perform.

"From a moral point of view, too, an occupied mind is necessary to banish dangerous longings, to counteract morbid sensibility, to withstand the wave of passion to which too many women succumb. A sound moral and intellectual training forearms a woman against the baneful effects of reading sensational novels and the bitter disillusionment which is commonly its sequel. A poor girl with her head full of the tender and wonderful things she has read in books is dismayed to find that they have no counterpart in real life. She would like to live like the heroines of these romances, always charming, always adorable, whose slightest whims are always gratified. What a grim awakening to come down from heights like those to the humdrum details of everyday domestic existence."

The three R's should be mastered by girls, plus a little knowledge of law and of history and always an acquaintance with the best in prose and poetry. Latin would be more profitable than Italian or Spanish; music and painting in cautious doses. Religious duties and household management, after all, came first in a woman's life. Economy and thrift without fussing over trifles were true virtues; no sense in economizing on candles and then letting a crafty steward cheat her out of large sums. "If a woman would gain the respect and obedience of her servants, she herself must have a practical knowledge of the details of cooking and housework. It is no good chiding a cook for taking too long to make an omelet, if you yourself don't know how long it should take; no good blaming her for putting too much sugar in the pudding if you haven't got the recipe at your finger tips." One wonders again whether Fénelon was not speaking here of his own thrifty mother, who was probably both a lady and a careful manager.

Sometimes the discipline of the priest speaks through the pedagogue, making stern demands on the parents rather than on the children. "One frequently demands of children a degree of punctuality and seriousness of which those who exact it would themselves be incapable. . . . Joy and confidence should be their children's ordinary condition; otherwise their minds are obscured and their spirits broken; if they be quick they are provoked to anger; if they be indolent they are stupefied. Fear is like those violent remedies which are used in cases of extreme illness; they purge but they impair the constitution and destroy the organs; a soul dominated by fear is always weakened thereby. It was by means of poetry and music that the principal sciences, the maxims of virtue, and the refinement of manners were introduced among the Hebrews, the Egyptians, and the Greeks . . ."

His is not the generalizing of a bystander, however. He has dealt with children, and young ones. "In the country they see a windmill and they want to know what it is; you must show them how the food that nourishes man is prepared. Further on they descry reapers; you must explain to them what they are doing, how the corn is sown, and how it grows in the earth. In the town they see shops, in which various crafts are practiced and diverse wares sold: you will then teach them by degrees the process of manufacture of all the articles which are used by man, and which commerce deals with. Little by little, and without special studies, they will learn the right way to make these things, and the exact value of each. This kind of knowledge is particularly interesting to girls."

This sort of teaching is certainly easier to describe than to practice; any parent knows that. And Fénelon might be accused of idealizing the adult-child relationship were it not that long after the writing of this treatise life called his hand and he was able to demonstrate his principles. Few facets of child interest escaped him. "You must give them well-bound books, even with gilt edges, and with beautiful pictures." He believed in teaching a child to write by letting him write about something that interested him, addressing the narration to a brother or cousin in the form of a note. He believed further that children thrived on short sessions. "Let their attention wander a little; from time to time even allow them to indulge in some recreation or games, in order that their minds may roam about freely; then bring them back by degrees to the end in view." He may have had different characteristics of the duchess's daughters in mind when he wrote that "lively and sensitive characters are prone to terrible excesses; but they often have great resources and often return from afar. . . . One has the wherewithal to interest them in what they are being taught but one has no hold over indolent natures. . . ."

Evidently he saw through the devices of the adolescent and may even have been irritated by some of his own sisters. "They have a natural facility for playing all sorts of parts; tears cost them nothing; their passions are strong and their knowledge is limited. . . . Girls are born with a violent desire to please; they are passionately fond of adornment; a headdress, a bit of ribbon, a curl placed higher or lower, the choice of a color— all these things are serious matters in their eyes. . . . Teach girls that the honor which comes from good conduct is more to be prized than that which comes from their hair and their ornaments." Even dress and hairdo come in for a share of comment, and the "noble simplicity" of the Greeks is commended.

Detailed though he sometimes may be, they are general principles of taste he is upholding and throughout the entire essay runs
the feeling that girls can be brought up to be noble women without becoming priggish, and happy women without frivolity.

Naturally, Fénelon had no way of knowing how far-reaching
would be the influence of this dissertation on the education of
girls, although no doubt he realized that in taking a stand ahead
of his time he was laying himself open to criticism; he may
even have preferred criticism to obscurity or he may have lost
himself in an honest cause, as he often did. At any rate, his
subject was relatively new, his style both forthright and charming, and in time the treatise reached the throne.

Letter writing occupied a considerable amount of Fénelon's
time throughout his life. Among his early letters none is more
often quoted than a letter written to his cousin, Marie Thérèse
Françoise, Marquise de Laval, shortly after he had become prior
of Carennac. He was thirty in the year 1681 when his uncle, the
bishop of Sarlat, resigned that benefice in his favor, thereby
adding to the young priest's income as well as to his dignity.
Evidently, when he visited his new holdings, the mood of May-
time was upon him and he himself not only greatly enjoyed
the scene but prolonged the pleasure by writing a humorously
ironic account of his visit.

Aye, madame, have no doubt about it; I am a man destined to come
on the scene with pomp and circumstance. You remember the magnificent reception your folk at Bellac gave me. Well, I'm not going to
tell you how I have been honored here. M. de Rouffillac, as representing

the nobility; M. Bosc, the curé, on behalf of the clergy; M. Rigaudie, the prior, for the monastic body; and finally, the local farmers, for the rest of the population, came all the way to Sarlat to offer me their greetings. And so I set forth in majesty, encompassed about by all these representatives. And now, behold me at the port of Carennac, the whole population packed in a dense crowd on the quay. Two boats, with the elite of the citizens on board, advance toward me and now I notice that, by a brave device, the doughtiest troops of the district are hidden away in a corner of the beautiful island you know so well. Thence they advance to greet me, marching in battle array, with much letting off of muskets. Instantly the air is darkened with smoke from all this firing, and naught is heard save alarming explosions of gunpowder. The mettlesome steed I was bestriding was for plunging into the river, but I, less enterprising than he, took my stand on *terra firma*. Then to the rattle of musketry is added the roll of drums. I cross the lovely Dordogne, which you can hardly see for the boats that are escorting mine. On shore a group of monks await me with grave and venerable mien. Their address is filled with the loftiest encomiums. My reply is suave and gentle, but not without a touch of the sublime.

The vast throng divides to yield me passage through their midst. Everyone scans me with searching eyes if haply he may read in mine what destiny awaits him. In this wise I make my way up toward the castle with slow and measured tread, so that I may offer myself yet a little longer to the inquisitive inspection of the public.

Meanwhile, from innumerable throats goes up the joyous shout: "He'll be the apple of our eye!"

And now behold me at the priory gates! The consuls address me through their mouthpiece, the orator-royal. That will tell you in what stately gems of eloquence, what rhetorical flights, the speech abounded. They liken me to the Sun. Anon, I am the Moon. Thereafter all the brightest stars have the honor of resembling me. From the stars we come to the elements, and thence to the meteors, and we finish up in happy style with the creation of the world. By this time the sun has gone to bed, and to set the seal on the likeness between us I retired to my room, and made ready to follow his example.

François de Fénelon

A few days later he wrote another letter in the same vein to the same cousin, describing his listening in on a case at law argued by the "local Ciceros." No doubt he listened with serious face but he reported with an ironic pen: "Needless to say, these learned gentlemen started with the creation of the world and went straight on through the flood, till they got to the matter at hand. The question at issue was whether bread was to be distributed to some children who had no bread to eat. Oh, what a strange twist of fortune. The advocate got plenty of praise; but the children got no bread. The hearing was adjourned; that is lawyers' jargon for telling the unlucky creatures that they've got to plead on an empty stomach. That much having been settled, the judges got up and went to lunch. I did likewise."

Perhaps his most solid intellectual work of that period was the writing of a tract to refute Malebranche's treatise on Nature and Grace. Malebranche at that time was near the height of his influence as a metaphysician; a few years later he was to be admitted as an honorary member to the Academy of Sciences. Born into high circles—his father was secretary to Louis XIII and one uncle a viceroy of Canada—he was given the best educational advantages and made good use of them. Deformed and constitutionally feeble, he withdrew from active life and gave himself without restraint to his philosophical and theological interests. After ten years' intensive study of Descartes he produced his great commentary, followed by other treatises both controversial and speculative. He was ordained a priest and remained a priest at heart although he never performed any parochial duties. Philosophically he remained a Cartesian although he differed widely from Descartes at certain points. He agreed with Descartes that physical bodies and individual minds were two separate classes of subjects but that in man the two substances coexist in unity. But God also is a substance, Malebranche contended, infinite and complete, depending on nothing else for its existence. It is the nature of this substance to be reasonable; indeed, it could not be otherwise, reasonableness being not an attribute but an essence of God. From the point of view of ethics, virtue becomes "the unique love of right reason" and self-love the root of all moral evil. Diligence consists in turning inward and by means of self-examination becoming attentive to the inward disclosure of right and wrong. Our senses, Malebranche argued, cannot yield knowledge of external bodies, any more than imagination can; our senses can only make us aware of states of mind that occur at the same time with certain physiological changes in the brain. Physical objects cannot cause our mind to know them because they are inferior in nature to the mind, because they are different in quality, because spatial distance of objects from the mind renders direct knowledge impossible, and because causal action between finite existents is impossible. Self-knowledge brings resignation; ultimately we realize our limitations and acquiesce in willing nothing because we can do nothing. "*Despectio sui* is the consequence of *inspectio sui.*" The further Malebranche pressed his thesis that God is essentially reason, order, law per se—unchangeable because he cannot change his own nature

[53]

and still be himself—the further removed he felt himself to be from God so that often he feared he might lose his God altogether.

Fénelon's refutation emphasized the point that God, however complete and perfect in himself, was also within reach of the least of his creatures and that their welfare was his deepest concern. God could not be imprisoned in his own laws, whether laws of his own nature or of man's. Fénelon would have none of the cold remoteness implicit in Malebranche's God; the God he knew and recognized was *at hand*, warmly accessible to all.

Bossuet, who gave Fénelon his assignment, was more than pleased with his young friend's dialectics, with his skillfully marshaled argument and felicity of expression. He might have been less satisfied if he had dreamed that a time would come when those same powers, sharpened by experience and made desperate in the cause of justice, would be turned against him.

In no other kind of writing except his letters does Fénelon show the warmth and passion of his nature that he shows in his sermons. Around the year 1687 he began to preach at different places, largely under the direction of Bossuet. Goulommiers, Etrépilly, La Ferté-sous-Jouarre, even the cathedral of Meaux itself, were included in his itinerary. There is a record in the cathedral noting that in 1684, during Lent, "an abbé named M. de La Mothe-Fénelon made an exhortation that was called a prayer." He often was seen with his friend Langeron or with Fleury in the coach of Bossuet as the latter drove about the countryside making his pastoral visits or returned to Germigny.

One of Fénelon's best known sermons was preached at court on the Feast of the Epiphany, in the presence of the ambassadors from Siam. The slim brown men in their silks and elaborate headdresses, coming from an Eastern world so much farther away then than now, must have added an exotic touch to the already gorgeous court.

Fénelon took his text from Isaiah 60:1 "Arise, shine; for thy light is come, and the glory of the Lord is risen upon thee," and uses it as a basis for discourse on the vocation of the Gentiles. First, he thanked God for allowing him to praise the work being done by the House of Foreign Missions in spreading the light of faith. "It fills my heart with joy to be speaking of the vocation of the Gentiles here in this House, whence men go forth to proclaim the glad tidings to those who have not heard them." Then he opened his argument, but continually gave way to apostrophe, glowing with the fervor of his own spirit. "O Spirit promised by the Fountain of all Truth to such as seek Thee, let my heart throb with this one longing, that it may draw Thee unto it and be filled with Thee. Dumb be my lips rather than that they should utter aught save Thy Word." For a time he traced the history of the church's expansion—"In the earliest times, St. Irenaeus and Tertullian showed that the church's sway was wider than the empire which claimed to embrace the earth. The wild and inaccessible regions to the north, which the sun scarce illumines with his ray, have beheld the heavenly light. The burning tides of Africa have been flooded with the tide of grace. Emperors, coming at last to adore the name they once reviled, have become the protectors of that very church whose blood they had caused to flow. The power of the gospel was not exhausted by these efforts. Time avails not to stay its onward course. It comes from Jesus Christ, and He is of all time." And then again description rose to wonder and became prayer. ". . . Let the fruit of Thy Word increase in those kingdoms to which Thou art sending it, but forget not Thine older Churches . . . Remember this Thy House and those who are trained in it to go forth into foreign lands, remember their tears, their prayers, their labours. . . . What shall I say to Thee, O Lord, of ourselves? . . . Take not from us, in the name of Thy Justice, the little faith which is still ours, but rather give it increase, purify it, and quicken it still more, so that it may lighten our darkness, stifle our passions, correct our judgment, to the end that having faithfully believed here below, we may hereafter behold in Thy bosom the everlasting object of our faith. *Amen*." His are works to which excerpts cannot do justice, since much of the sermons' moving power lies in their alteration of mood, their spontaneous breaking into prayers of contrition and longing, their recurrent notes of praise and thanksgiving.

Another literary product of this mid-period of Fénelon's thinking, although written a little later, is his *Dialogue Concerning Eloquence in General, And particularly that kind which is fit for the Pulpit*. In the English translation of William Stevenson, rector of Morningthorp in Norfolk, in 1722, the translator comments: "Some Apology, however, may be expected for my Undertaking a Translation that deserv'd the finest Pen. All I can say, without the Appearance of Vanity, is, that I was afraid it shou'd fall into worse Hands." The French editor comments in his preface: "Both the Antients and the Moderns have treated Eloquence, with different views, and in different Ways; as Logicians, as Grammarians, and as Criticks; but we still wanted an Author who should handle this delicate Subject as a Philosopher, and a Christian; and this the late Archbishop of Cambray has done in the following Dialogues." Then he comments further: "They who value nothing but Wit, will probably dislike the Plainness of these Dialogues: but they wou'd form another Judgment of them if they consider'd that there are different Styles of Dialogue; of which Antiquity furnishes us with two celebrated Patterns; the Dialogues of Plato; and those of Lucian. Plato like a true Philosopher, study'd chiefly to give Force and Light to his Arguments; and chose no other Stile than what is us'd in Conversation: so that his Language is artless, easy and familiar. On the contrary Lucian is every-where witty and sparkling. All the Persons he introduced have a sprightly delicate Fancy; so that in reading him, we forget the feign'd Characters of Gods and Men who speak in his Dialogues; and cannot but see the ingenious Author in everything they say. We must own however that he is an Original, who has succeeded wonderfully in this way of writing. He ridicul'd man in the most facetious pleasing Manner: While Plato instructed them with Gravity and Wisdom. The Archbishop of Cambray has imitated them both, on different subjects. In his Dialogues of the Dead (which he compos'd for the Instruction of a young Prince that was his

Pupil), we find the various Wit and agreeable Humour of Lucian. And in the following Sheets, where he lays down the Rules of such a grave Eloquence as is proper to move and persuade Men; he imitates Plato: everything is natural, and instructive; and instead of Wit and Humour we find Truth and Wisdom shine throughout the Composure."

These are dialogues to be read in leisurely fashion in order to be most enjoyed because the asides, not particularly quotable in themselves, are often the life of the discourse. Frequently they have the flavor of today; especially in their speculation about what a pulpit ought to be. B remarks to A, "I was charm'd with my Preacher. You had a great loss, Sir, in not hearing him. I have hired a Pew, that I may not miss one of his Lent-Sermons. If you did but once hear him, you cou'd never bear any other." To which A replies, "If it be so, I'm resolv'd never to hear him. I wou'd not have any One Preacher give me a distaste of all Others; on the contrary, I shou'd chuse one that will give me such a Relish and Respect for the Word of God, as may dispose me the more to hear it preach'd every where." And then the two are off, with C to urge them on. "Now you have begun, Sir," says C, "I hope you will go on with this useful Subject." As if B needed urging! That is why he is here on these pages "to give us some general notion of the Harangue" he has heard in his favorite pulpit.

Easily and smoothly Fénelon makes his way among the ancients. "Demosthenes moves, warms, and captivates the Heart. He was too sensibly touch'd with the Interest of his Country, to mind the little glittering Fancies that amus'd

[58]

Isocrates. Every oration of Demosthenes is a close Chain of Reasoning, that represents the Notion of a Soul who disdains any Thought that is not great. His Discourses gradually increase in Force by greater Light and New Reasons; which are always illustrated by bold Figures and lively Images. One cannot but see that he has the good of the Republic entirely at heart; and that Nature itself speaks in all his Transports; for his artful Address is so masterly, that it never appears. Nothing ever equalled the Force and Vehemence of his Discourses. Have you never read the Remarks that Longinus made on them, in his treatise on the Sublime?" Of course B never has read them, so that A is able to inform him why he thinks it surpasses Aristotle's *Rhetoric*.

Continually Fénelon presses home a point he was to make over and over in different contexts all his life: to be natural is the height of artistry as well as the most convincing procedure. "But we must further conclude that to paint well, we must imitate Nature; and observe what she does when she is left to herself; and is not constrain'd by Art . . . Now doth a Man naturally use many Gestures when he says common Things, without Vehemence, or the least mixture of any form of Passion?" B admits that he does not. "On such common Subjects, then, we ought not to use any Action in public Discourses, or at least but little . . . nay there are some Occasions where an Orator might best express his Thoughts by Silence. For if, being full of some great Sentiment, he continue immovable for a Moment; this surprising Pause wou'd keep the Minds of the Audience in suspence, and express an Emotion too big for Words to utter." So speaks the preacher who knows what it is to be stirred by his own eloquence and to plumb depths of spirit, his own and the audience's, for which there are no words.

The man who wrote this discourse would be labeled by a modern a finished orator. "In order to make a lasting Impression on People's Minds, we must support their attention by moving their Passions: For dry Instructions can have but little Influence." This is the same pedagogy couched in terms of adult interest that he had earlier expressed regarding the instruction of children. "If you must employ Art, conceal it so well under an exact Imitation, that it may pass for Nature itself. But to speak the Truth, Orators in such Cases, are like Poets who write Elegies or other passionate Verses; they must feel the Passion they describe, else they can never paint it well. . . .

"Consider then, the Advantages that a Preacher must have who does not get his Sermon by-heart. He is entirely Master of himself; he speaks in an easy unaffected way; and not like a formal Declaimer. Things flow from their proper Source. . . . Everything shou'd tend to make the Hearers in love with what is truly Great and Good . . . An Orator then shou'd have nothing either to hope, or fear, from his Hearers, with regard to his own Interest." Speaking of the love of moderation, frugality, a generous concern for the public good, and an inviolable regard of the laws and constitution, he makes this searching observation: "The Orator's zeal for these must appear in his Conduct as well as in his Discourses."

This author is a man who knows the discipline of spoken

instruction. "A Division (in his discourse) chiefly relieve's the Speaker's Memory. And even this Effect might be much better contain'd by following a natural Order without any express Division: for the true Connection of Things best directs the Mind."

With him, as with any creative mind, the arts instruct one another. A asks, "Do you love quavering notes in Musick? Are you not better pleas'd with those brisk significant Notes that describe Things, and express the Passions?" To which B replies, "Quavers are no Use: they only amuse the Ear and don't affect the Mind. Our Musick was once full of them; and was therefore very weak and confus'd: but now we begin to refine our taste, and come nearer to the Musick of the Ancients: which is a kind of passionate Declamation, that acts powerfully upon the Soul." Then A responds. "There ought to be a kind of Eloquence in Musick itself; and in both these Arts we ought to reject all false and thrilling Beauties." So with architecture. "Did you not notice the Roses, Holes, unconnected Ornaments, and disjointed little Knacks that these Gothick Buildings are full of? These odd Conceits are just such Beauties in Architecture as forc'd Antitheses and Quibbles are in Eloquence." Evident here is that distaste for the Gothic as barbarous which was characteristic of Fénelon's period as well as the early eighteenth century. As mountains were not beautiful but "horrid" and unpleasing, so the aspiring spires and vertical lines spoke a language unknown to the age of the le Grand Monarque. Order, dignity, the golden mean—such was the word of the day.

"It happens but too often (as I heard an ingenious Lady observe) that our Preachers speak Latin, in English. The most essential Quality of a good Preacher is to be instructive: but he must have great Abilities and Experience to make him so . . . One might follow some Preachers twenty Years, without getting sufficient Knowledge of Religion." He wants the scriptures taught with due regard for their content and intrinsic significance. "It mangles the Scripture thus to shew it to Christians only in separate Passages. And however great the Beauty of such Passages may be, it can never be fully perceived unless one knows the Connection of them . . . Sometimes Preachers preposterously quote the Scripture only for the sake of Decency of Ornament: and it is not then regarded as the Word of God; but as the Invention of Men."

A pastor's is the highest of callings, he feels, and it takes more than preaching, however eloquent, to make a true pastor. "While a Priest, who ought to be a *Man of God and thoroughly furnished unto all good Works,* shou'd be diligent in rooting out Ignorance and Offences from the Field of the Church; I think it unworthy of him to waste his Time in his Closet, in smoothing Periods, giving delicate touches to his Descriptions; and inventing quaint Divisions." Frankly, B thinks S. Austin "the most jingling Quibbler that ever wrote," but A, admitting the criticism, feels that S. Austin had something more important even than eloquence. "He knew the Heart of Man entirely well . . . All his Works plainly show his Love of God." Then A sums up the matter for Fénelon: "Gentlemen, good night. I'll leave you with these words of S. Jerome to Nepotian,

'When you teach in the Church, don't endeavor to draw Applause, but rather Sighs and Groans from the People: let their Tears praise you. The Discourses of a Clergyman shou'd be full of the Holy Scripture. Be not a Declaimer, but a true Teacher of the Mysteries of God."

It would be impossible to understand the Fénelon of the first years of his maturity, when he spoke from the vigor of his fourth decade before he knew the rigors of persecution, without becoming saturated with his writings, for in them his reasoned opinion is set down deliberately with intention to instruct and persuade and with all the warmth, humor, and love of his fellows which served to draw to him people of all circumstances and all temperaments.

*I*nto the *W*orld

WHEN the Abbé de Fénelon came to Versailles in 1689
the era of great victories of the early part of the reign
of Louis XIV was passing; the crushing price of war was being
felt more and more acutely; public discontent and misery continued to increase as under the glittering surface of Versailles
the fiber of French life was rotting out.

Colbert had conceived the state as a vast machine, every part
of which received its impetus from the outside—and that
impetus was Colbert himself. He said, in substance, private
initiative was not to be trusted; liberty vitiates efficiency. "France
is like an old rusty machine, that still spins around from the
impetus given it long ago, but it will break in pieces at the first
collision," wrote Fénelon a few years later. But Colbert had
complacently set to work on the tottering machine. He got all
the parts under control—finance, industry, commerce, fine arts,

navy, colonies, administrations, fortifications, and even the law. Colbert, however, was never more than the mechanic of the king's carriage.

The king's political pattern was an acquisitive one. He had a passion for tearing down his barns and building greater ones. The sole business of his minister was to provide ever greater resources for such sacrifices. But there were times when the king was aware of vague whisperings that made him uneasy, "This night—thy soul." These two sides of Louis XIV's nature were represented by his two most intimate advisers. These two advisers were inimical to each other and each was bent on annihilating the other. One was Louvois, his minister of war, a man more cruel and sensuous, more extravagant and greedy than Louis himself. Louvois was a reflection of the king. He was disdainful of the world, he was arrogant and violent with everyone except Louis XIV—to whom he was pliant and flattering, dangling before him the glory of war and the power of dominion, or tempting him to extravagant building. The other was Mme. de Maintenon, who stood for the king's obligation to the Divine. She endeavored to embody his conscience; reminding him to be devout in his worship and faithful in his observance of religious forms.

Louis XIV was able for the most part to keep these two conflicting elements of his nature and his affairs in separate compartments. However, in one fatal act they met—the Revocation of the Edict of Nantes. This act, which incidentally marked the beginning of the ruin of Colbert's fine machinery, was an invasion into the domain of the conscience of his people where no monarch had ever ventured with safety. It precipitated the breakdown of that precarious uniformity achieved by Richelieu and Colbert—a fact which neither Louis XIV nor his ministers would permit themselves to recognize but for which they compensated by an accentuated severity and an excess of regimentation.

If Fénelon had not already been aware of the dissolution in progress, his association with Colbert's daughters, the Duchesses de Beauvilliers and de Chévreuse, would soon have informed him. The breaking up of France was only too obvious. The poverty of the people, disease and famine, crushing taxes and extortions, official debasement of currency, bankruptcy, increase in state prisons, suppression of all institutions that guarded state rights, the monstrous and inveterate luxury at Versailles —all testified to the decadence of France.

Warfare itself had passed from a gallant defense of national rights to an efficient instrument for human suffering whereby greater revenues could be acquired for the king. The War of the Spanish Succession was Louis XIV's last war of aggrandizement. For the first time military conscription was resorted to; severe discipline by superior officers was authorized; the king furnished uniform clothing and equipment to the army; the bayonet became an acceptable weapon and the status of the infantry was raised thereby; the organization of grenadiers was an innovation, and the galleys were perfected. Colbert had systematized their production to such a degree that he was producing one a day but could not find men to man them. Therefore the common form of punishment became the galleys.

Colbert urged the judges to sentence every offender to this living death; vagrants were kidnaped and short-time offenders held for life to this grueling business. Galley slavery became one of France's dark shadows.

Then, too, during Louis XIV's reign, the burning and destruction of cities not in the path of invasion was permitted. Marshal Durac, in 1689, was the first to involve France in this depredation. He proposed to destroy all the cities in the neighborhood of the Rhine between him and his objective, every burg and village. After the fatal permission had been given him, however, he would have abandoned the outrage but Louvois would not permit this withdrawal. Speyer, Worms, Oppenheim, Frankenthal, Bingen, were condemned to the flames. The inhabitants were given the privilege of emigrating to France but could not return to their own country. License and rape by the invading army was, as in earlier wars, unhindered by the officers. A plea had been made to preserve the cathedrals at Worms and Speyer and what personal property the inhabitants could store in them. This was denied. The beautiful Rhineland countryside became a mass of smoking ruins, as it periodically has in the centuries that have followed. The first desolation, however, carried with it more tragedy because it opened the door to violence, and sowed seeds of resentment that have never been uprooted. Voltaire remarked the beginning of bombing during this period: "Louis XIV was revenged upon Algiers by means of a new art . . . this wonderful but terrible art was that of bomb-vessels by means of which maritime towns may be burnt to ashes . . . but the art, which was afterward carried to other nations, only served to multiply human calamities; and more than once became terrible to France where it was invented."

Over the poverty and misery of war was laid the veneer of Versailles. Its magnificence was deliberately designed to weaken the nobility and waste the money of the ambitious merchant class. The universal debt, the semiruined estates, the tottering finances of many aristocratic families are revealed in the correspondence of the day. It was universal and fashionable to ruin oneself at court, almost a sure passport to royal favor. Articles of luxury began to pass into the hands of the middle class and great bankers and merchants were able to buy their way into the most highly born families. The nobility was imitated in manners and customs, the pretty daughters of opulent bourgeois married ruined heirs of dukes and marquises.

The cultural life of the day, or at least its social façade, is faithfully perpetuated in the Gobelin tapestries, especially in the series depicting the history of Louis XIV. One interesting scene shows the final result of a long quarrel over precedence between the French and Spanish ambassadors. The Roi Soleil won out, as he was at this period winning on all fronts. On the tapestry the Spanish are presented as dully clad figures, subdued in air, huddled on a lower level than the king of France and his ministers, with the court gathered about them. The tapestries are endlessly instructive. One sees everywhere the heavy rather handsome face of Louis XIV with its long nose, brown eyes, slightly receding chin—the Bourbon profile at its best—framed in the great curling wig, the whole set off by laces, and raised above his fellows by high-heeled shoes.

The king had a vigorous and robust physique, he was fond of eating and exercising, particularly of dancing and riding. All such activities he performed with dignity; there was about him a trace of Spanish punctiliousness and courtesy. He was said to be always "erect without stiffness." He enjoyed taking part in ballets, attired in mythological costume.

The personality and character of Louis XIV have been the subject of endless and intensive dispute among historians and students of French civilization, up to the present-day theory of the monarchist school of thought; these protagonists take the stand that the great king was indubitably a great man. It seems likely that the early insecurity of the boy-king's life, as he moved through Europe at the heels of his armies, must have influenced the mature psychology of the all-powerful ruler. Modern analytical science, which places such enormous emphasis on the earliest years of life, would see in the obsession with power, luxury and grandeur of the king's later reign, also perhaps in the multiplicity of love affairs, a compensation for the anxieties and disappointments of boyhood. Louis XIV lived and moved in a cloud of incense. A hint of criticism, unsolicited suggestion, was unbearable. Could there be the faintest shadow on the glory of the sun?

This was a time of great outward accomplishment. Paris rose in stately buildings and spread in dignified planning; the great south façade of the Louvre, the sober elegance of the Place Vendôme, the fine dome of the Invalides, the exquisite stone lacework of the Sainte-Chapelle, and the great mass of Versailles itself—in fact, many of the buildings and settings that are the very essence of Paris were either constructed in full or were in progress during this period.

The extraordinary circle of literary talent, rising to genius in the names of Racine, Molière, Corneille, La Fontaine and Saint-Simon, is both a product of this period and a directive force in it. Architects, landscape gardeners, sculptors, furniture makers, jewelers, the practitioners of the hundred and one smaller arts that add to comfort and decorative elegance, the embellishers in general of the art of living, all reached an astonishing height of refinement. The golden jeweled snuffbox, the great Sèvres vases, the exquisite toys of enamel and gold are all familiar to us. The brocaded silks and satins and the opulent curves of the court furniture are the familiar appendages of this expansive era. It was a time when large plain surfaces were disdained; more and richer garlands, armorial designs, emblems, more luscious cherubs and goddesses appeared in palace and official decorations. In painting Mignard and Nattier, in contrast to the Spanish Velasquez and El Greco, give the effect of competence and skill rather than the originality of genius. But the engravings of Nanteuil weighted the scales somewhat more heavily on the side of French art, as did the calm and classical landscapes of Poussin and Lorrain, neither of whom was a court painter—indeed they worked far from Versailles.

Fénelon detested meaningless complications and tasteless multiplicity, the superfluous piling up of useless masses. The luxurious extravagance of dress, the great towering wigs, and the elaborate coiffures were abhorrent to him. His discriminating taste longed for a return to the flowing simplicity of the Greek garments. The Abbé Galet says that Fénelon's wardrobe was always a very simple, scanty one, made up of the simplest materials, even his ecclesiastical vestments were devoid of lace and other costly trimmings. One day he showed the abbé a fine pastoral cross set with emeralds which the elector of Cologne had given him. The abbé admired its richness and suggested to Fénelon that he wear it. But he set it aside as inappropriate, saying the cross was a memorial to the poverty and nakedness of Jesus and should not be insulted by worldly ornamentation. Simple appropriateness was his reply to the artificiality and superfluity in art and literature.

To the average courtier the inordinately stiff and elaborate costumes, the immense wigs, the endless hours of senseless waiting about in drafty anterooms involved in court life, the lack of privacy, the tedium of etiquette, must have been a heavy price to pay for royal recognition.

But not to be seen at court was to be forgotten and even in some cases to incur the ill will of the sovereign; Louis XIV expected his nobles to be always at hand, ever ready for the possible word or smile. Undoubtedly there were brilliant gatherings; the wit of Saint-Simon, the amiable grace of Mme. de Sévigné, the dignified presence of Bossuet, Bishop of Meaux, the allusions of the literary, the wit of the philosophers— all these must have afforded much of interest to the soberly inclined. For the frivolous there was the impetuous gaiety of the young duchesses, first of Henriette d'Orléans; later the sprightly Duchess of Burgundy, the attractions of the pretty maids of honor, the graces of the silk-clad ladies, and the spice of intrigue. There was hunting in the nearby forests of Fontainebleau and Saint-Germain; there was gaming for high stakes; there was dancing—though at court functions it was strictly ruled by etiquette; there were plays in which Molière spread his witty satires before the courtiers; there were festivals, routs, and gorgeous divertissements galore. And, finally, the court was the place to make one's fortune.

It was into such a world that the Abbé de Fénelon emerged as a significant figure. Many in court already knew this young priest, who seemed as devoted as he was brilliant, as sternly demanding of the great as of the humble, whose way of life was an open book and a challenging, even a disconcerting one to courtiers often tired of frivolity. Fénelon had a quiet independence, an intrinsic dignity and great charm, so that his presence added yet another facet to the brilliant assembly.

What was the meaning of Versailles for Fénelon? What did he think of the king? What did he think of the men and women who were functionaries in the court, and what did he think of his own relationship to this vicissitude of his life? His attitude toward the king was a remarkable one, combining at once a tremendous, almost spiritual respect for the monarchy, a feeling almost of awe, with a genuinely upright and independent spirit. It was during the early years of his residence at Versailles that the famous *Letter to the King* came from his pen. There is no evidence that it ever fell into the hands of

Louis XIV and it possibly was never intended for his perusal, but was written rather as an analysis of the political situation for the author and the close friends at the Hôtel de Beauvilliers. But whatever its purpose might have been, it does reveal the insight of its writer. After enumerating the evils that were overtaking France with its wars of vengeance, and calling the attention of his Majesty to his subjects dying of hunger, the abandonment of the soil and ruined business and commerce, he says, "France has become a huge hospital. . . . You alone have brought all this trouble on yourself; for, the whole kingdom having been ruined, you now hold everything in your own hands, and no one can so much as live save by your bounty. . . . The people who once loved you so deeply are beginning to lose affection, confidence, and even respect. Sedition is being kindled little by little on all sides. . . . If, they say, the king has the heart of a Father toward his people, it will be more to his glory to give them bread. . . . You do not love God; even your fear for him is a slavish fear. It is hell you dread. Your religion consists only of superstitions, and little superficial practices. You make everything center around your own person, as if you were the God of the whole earth."

Yet it was to this very monarch, who could not tolerate independence in his subjects, that years later the dying Fénelon could pay a significant tribute to the personal dominion Louis XIV exercised over France, saying there was never a moment when he did not have deep gratitude and ardent zeal for the person of the king.

Then, again, we see Fénelon fascinated by the court even

while he is struggling against attachment to it. He loved the flash of keen wit and the zeal of clever argument to be found there. His correspondence fifteen years after his departure from its splendor bears traces of his nostalgia. He was allured by it or he would not have cherished such keen memories of it throughout his lifetime. But even at the time of his highest popularity he wrote to a close friend of his attempt to be free of its demands upon him: "I feel myself to be embarked on a rapid river, which is flowing toward the land to which I go; the essential thing that I must do is not to seize hold of anything, not to catch at the branches, or the sand, or the rocks that border the way. The course of the river forms my own course; the only thing is that I must not let myself stop; I must always allow myself to be carried along without becoming distracted, either in contradictions, amusements, or aridity. . . . All this is only the bank that one discovers in passing, where one can only succeed in not halting for a moment by not stiffening oneself against the current of grace."

But beneath the veneer and superficiality of the courtiers' lives he found the same need that had called forth his compassion in the old Saint-Sulpice days. The pain of the bored and weary men and women about the court was no less real to him than the exigencies of the poverty-stricken souls of his first parish:

"The poor man who has not bread to eat finds a leaden cross in his poverty, and God mingles troubles in his cup very much akin to those in the cup of the prosperous. The rich man hungers for freedom and ease and the poor man hungers for bread; and

Into the World

whereas the latter can freely knock at any door and call upon
any passer-by for pity, the man of high estate is ashamed to
seek compassion or relief. It is God's good pleasure thus to
confound human greatness which is really no more than disguised powerlessness. . . . You know by experience that court
favor can give no real happiness."

And again he wrote out of his court experience: "The trials
of high position are more acute than rheumatism or headache.
But religion turns them all to good account; it teaches us to
look upon all such things as a mere bondage and in the patient
acceptance thereof it shows us a real freedom, which is all the
more real because it is hidden from outer gaze."

At this time Mme. de Maintenon's influence with Louis XIV
was at its height and he was making valiant efforts toward
moral reform. He was past fifty years of age and was beginning
to be wearied by the superficial routine of the court, and he had
no desire that his grandchildren should follow in his own
unsteady path. He was through with the intrigues and jealousies
in which his former mistresses had kept him embroiled. Mme.
de Montespan had been a haughty and avaricious woman reject-
ing all that might savor of spirituality. Her striking arrogance
and imperious ways had succeeded in winning the enmity of
both nobles and clergy while at the same time it supplied
spice to the daily gossip among the courtiers. For ten years she
had outfaced competitors for the king's affection and attention
until Mme. de Maintenon's insidious and quiet charm and
dignity and passion for religion had at last awakened the king

[75]

to the fact that he had a conscience. Her cool and even temper rested him after the storms of Mme. de Montespan. His conversion however, had nothing to do with his reason nor did it bear any fruit in magnanimity. Throughout his life his religious activity was tinged with bigotry. Nevertheless, it did begin to change the tone of the court. Religious observances became a fashion and the splendid gaiety of the earlier years was being gradually thrown aside and a decorous dullness began to dim the brilliance. This sober emphasis on life had stirred Louis to interest himself in the education of his children and especially of his grandson, who might himself become king.

Through the influence of such advisers as Mme. de Maintenon and the Duc de Beauvilliers, Fénelon was appointed preceptor to the young Duke of Burgundy. It is doubtful whether, ten years earlier, Louis XIV would have appointed a man of Fénelon's character to the position of tutor to his grandson with all the privileges and responsibilities accruing to court life. Bossuet had, of course, been tutor to the dauphin, but the colorless heir apparent was no such problem as the Duke of Burgundy, nor was Bossuet for all his uprightness so demanding a spiritual adviser as Fénelon. However, Louis both admired Fénelon's erudition and clung a little wistfully to his idealism. Early in his relationship with the young priest he had once remarked, "l'esprit le plus beau et le plus chimérique de mon royaume"—the finest and most visionary mind in my kingdom. He even found confidence in Fénelon's level gaze, accustomed as he was to living and moving before adoring eyes.

Naturally Fénelon's friends congratulated him on his new

honors; their enthusiasm was tremendous and strengthened his own confidence in the appropriateness of his calling. Only M. Tronson, so far as the record goes, felt the dangers and temptations of his new surroundings. He wrote to the younger man from the fullness of his conviction on the matter. The letter has the ring of a father advising a beloved son:

Perhaps you have been surprised, monsieur, to miss me from the crowd of those who congratulate you on the honor his Majesty has just done you . . . I thought that in a matter which concerns me so deeply, I could not but begin by praising God for His care of you, and asking Him to continue His mercies towards you . . . And I can now assure you of the real joy it gave me to hear you had been chosen.

. . . His Majesty has given you the charge of an education which is so important to the welfare of the state and the good of the Church, that if one is a Frenchman and a Christian one must rejoice to see it in good hands.

But I candidly acknowledge that there is much apprehension mingled with my pleasure in view of the dangers to which you are exposed; because it cannot be denied that, in the natural course of events, promotion makes the way of salvation harder; it opens the door to the prizes of the world, but beware lest it close it on the enduring gains of Heaven. Doubtless you can do great good in your new post, but you may also be guilty of much evil: there is no medium under such conditions; success or failure will have incalculable consequence . . . You now live among people whose conversation is practically pagan . . . you will find yourself surrounded by everything calculated to indulge the senses and awaken dormant passions; it will require great grace and great faith to withstand such impressions. A very short time suffices to make familiar maxims seem exaggerated, however confident of them you might be when you thought of them at the foot of the Cross . . .

If you ever need study and meditation on the Bible, it is now; until now you have looked to it to strengthen you with Truth, and inspire you with good thoughts; now you will need it to banish evil ones and shield you from lies.

. . . There are some who make no effort for advancement, but nevertheless remove such obstacles as might hinder it. They do not curry favor with the influential, but they are not averse to making the best impression; it is the little human self-revelations that often win advancement, and thus no man may feel that he had no part in his own promotion. Exhibitions of wit, though they may be almost unconscious, are to be shunned; it is better to crush them beneath contrition and humility of heart.

You will perhaps esteem my letter somewhat over free and over long; it may seem a misplaced sermon rather than an apt congratulation. I should be more brief and less outspoken if I were not so eager for your welfare . . . After so many finished compliments as you will have received, you have enough to counterbalance my plain speaking.

It was no easy assignment the king gave to Fénelon in appointing him tutor to this particular prince. Saint-Simon, never too reliable, was none the less a daily visitant at court and his impressions are not without value, especially when there was nothing at stake in his relationship to an individual. He was, however, both malicious and cynical. He has recorded his appraisal of the young prince: "The Duke of Burgundy was born terrible, and in his early youth he made everyone tremble. Hard and irascible even to the utmost passion, incapable of bearing the slightest resistance without flying into a rage which made people fear that his physical frame would entirely give way—all these states I myself have often witnessed; obstinate to excess, passionately fond of every kind of pleasure, of good food, of hunting with fury, and of music with a sort of rapture. Intellect and penetration sparkled from him on every side; his repartees astonished; his replies always tended toward correctness and depth; the most abstract knowledge was child's play to him."

This was the boy whom the Duc de Beauvilliers and Fénelon had undertaken to make into a man—a man and a king. Saint-Simon continued: "The marvel is that in a very short space of time, devotion and grace made quite another being of him, and changed his many and dreadful faults into the entirely opposite virtues. From this abyss a Prince was seen to issue, at once affable, gentle, humane, generous, patient, modest, humble, and severe towards himself. Henceforth, he thought only of combining his duties, as son and subject, with those to which he saw himself destined."

Here was a task for any teacher. Occupied as Fénelon was with many other duties, especially as spiritual adviser to those whose place in life made their spiritual well-being highly important, he consistently put the education of the young prince ahead of every other consideration. The Abbé Fleury was entrusted with a large part of the instruction, assisted by the Abbé de Langeron and Père de Valois, but it was Fénelon who directed the course of study. Among Abbé Fleury's papers, a syllabus has been found, written in Fénelon's hand:

1695: "I think the Duke of Burgundy should be allowed to continue, during the remainder of this year, his compositions and translations, as he is doing them at present. The compositions are taken from Ovid's Metamorphoses; the subject offers much variety; it teaches a great many Latin words and idiomatic expressions; it amuses him, and, since composition is a most thorny study, as much amusement as possible should be introduced into it. . . . He enjoys them immensely and nothing could be more profitable either from the point of view of his Latin, or of the development of his taste."

That the young prince found his Latin amusing not only implies the skill of an excellent teacher, who could turn such tasks into amusement, but also foreshadows the future dauphin, who was more a master of letters than a master of affairs. In those early years the teacher observed his own wise precept "to follow and assist nature." In later years his efforts to instill strength of character were more insistent. For the archbishop from Cambrai and the Duc de Beauvilliers at Versailles never gave up their ambition to make of this grandson of Louis XIV the great and good king they conceived of as being France's only hope. His studies, his amusements, his opinions, his personal relationships came constantly under their scrutiny. Mme. de Maintenon herself observed that if the Duke of Burgundy had faults it was not for lack of counselors. Yet as the years passed he constantly revealed to them a man who shunned responsibility as a leader and fell far short of being a clever courtier. In those later years Fénelon wrote: "Your piety tries to govern an army like a nunnery, and wears itself out on trifling details while it neglects everything essential to your honor and the glory of the arms of France."

In the beginning, however, when Fénelon was instructing a seven-year-old-child, his moral admonitions were more subtle and sprang out of the mouths of those creatures, even fauns, bees and flies who lived in the *Fables* conjured for him. These *Fables* are listed among the classic ones although they lack the sharp wit and brilliant writing of LaFontaine, whom their writer admired. The *Fables* had humor and emotion, brevity and grace. In them the young duke's sense of humor was called into play against his own faults. As in this one: "The child Bacchus was learning to read and was annoyed by an old Faun who laughed at his mistakes; 'How dare you make fun of the son of Jove?' exclaimed the angry little god. The disrespectful Faun replied unmoved: 'How dare the son of Jove make mistakes?'"

Or there is the fable of Master Whimsical. "What has happened to Melanthus? . . . There is a wrinkle in his stocking this morning and we all shall have to suffer for it. He cries, he roars, he makes a noise, he moves to pity. . . . We must not be silent, we must not talk, we must not laugh, we must not be sad. Now he has changed again he avows his fault, laughs at his own absurdities, and imitates them to our amusement. You would think he would never lose his temper again—you are wrong, there will be another outbreak soon."

Fénelon and the Abbé de Fleury, the Abbé de Langeron and Père de Valois banded together never to flatter their pupil, nor to overlook his faults and errors, but at the same time never to remonstrate in anger and always to try to win the boy's co-operation rather than threatening or forcing him. They made it a habit to blame themselves whenever blame was due, quickly to ask pardon when pardon was due, and to keep silent when the boy's anger drove him to outbursts in which reason was useless. Fénelon was never above admitting himself in the wrong. D'Alembert recounts an incident in his

Eloge de Fénelon which must have occurred in the early six-teen-nineties after Louis XIV had given Fénelon the abbey of Saint-Valéry and made him almoner to the king: "Father Seraphin, a Capuchin, a missionary more zealous than eloquent, was preaching before Louis XIV. The abbé, then almoner to the king, was at sermon and fell asleep. Father Seraphin, perceiving it, suddenly interrupted his discourse, calling out 'Wake that sleeping abbé, whose only apparent motive for coming here is to pay court to the king.'" Then d'Alembert comments: "Féne-lon liked to relate this anecdote, and with real satisfaction praised the preacher, who had shown so much apostolic liberty; and the king, by whose silence it was approved."

A completely spoiled seven-year-old boy can be a match for any but the wisest adult. Saint-Simon says of the prince that "he was so impetuous as to desire to break the clocks when they struck the hour summoning him to do something he did not like and fell into the most extraordinary fury against the rain when it interfered with his desires. Opposition threw him into a pas-sion, as I have often been witness in his early childhood." But a nature so tempestuous was also ardent in its affection. No doubt the child realized that he was happier under Fénelon's stern and loving discipline, warmed by the genuine concern and understanding of his tutor, than he had ever been when allowed to do as he pleased. There are two little notes in existence which show the child's struggle to conquer his faults.

"I promise, on my word as a prince, to M. l'Abbé de Féne-lon, to do what he tells me immediately, and to obey him directly he forbids me to do anything; and if I break it I accept any kind of punishment and disgrace. Delivered at Versailles, November 29, 1689. Signed, Louis."

But it is difficult for even the most robust determination to remain resolute. The second note attests a fresh start: "Louis, who promises afresh to keep my promise better. This 20th of September. I beseech M. de Fénelon to take it again." Evidently he failed repeatedly. On one occasion his old native tempestuousness came uppermost and he refused to obey an order with the sharp exclamation, "No, no, sir! I remember who I am and who you are!" The next day, when the boy's anger had cooled, Fénelon went to him and gravely explained who the boy really was—an ignorant, undisciplined child—and who he himself was, respecting his own knowledge with all simplicity and dignity. Lest the prince in the boy think the priest was currying favor by remaining in a post where his instruction was not met with regard, he would ask the boy to accompany him to the king, while he, Fénelon, asked his Majesty to release him from his post. There is small doubt that he meant what he said and only the most earnest protestations of the little prince, abetted by Mme. de Maintenon, caused him to withdraw the suggestion.

The training of a prince consisted in more than lessons or persuasion toward ethical conduct. M. de Louville, in his memoirs, 1696, describes the daily life of the young princes:

They lived plainly, being allowed only dry bread in the morning, but as much as they liked of the simple food served them at dinner and supper. They kept Lent more or less according to their age, Monseigneur de Bourgogne having begun to observe it scrupulously. As for their other rules, no citizen of Paris would risk such a system. They wear nothing on their heads even when riding or when it rains. They go out daily, whatever be the weather, and take violent exercise, sometimes when at Fontainebleau, remaining out the whole day.

The hardening system is due to M. de Beauvilliers, who believes that an infirm prince is useless, especially in France, where he is called upon to lead his army . . . So far it has succeeded admirably.

They rise at 7.45 and go to Mass, then to the levee of the Dauphin for a moment, then to the king, remaining till 9.30. From 10 to 12 they study. Then they dine together, and amuse themselves in their own apartments until 2.45. In summer they study till 5; in winter they spend the same time out of doors. At 8 they sup, and afterwards play at indoor games until about 9.

They go out together, and three or four young lords with them; but they are alone the rest of the day. They are forbidden to whisper to each other but must always speak out to everyone.

On Sundays and fete-days their lessons are religious, but they keep the same hours. At Fontainebleau they have some degree of holidays. M. de Fénelon has a horror of pedantry, and dwells chiefly on the study of politics, history, and military tactics. The object is to teach them everything that is beautiful and curious and useful in all arts and sciences, but nothing to be specialized, a definite pursuit being regarded as unworthy and ridiculous in a prince.

Monseigneur de Bourgogne had to work harder than the others. Histories were drawn up for him, and he was required to join in discussions on the policy of foreign rulers and of the earlier French kings. He had an extraordinary memory for dates and chronology.

They were punished rigorously, being sent to bed or kept indoors, but never whipped. They never required punishment over their lessons.

It was the immensity of the power that would one day fall into the hands of these young princes that made their education so important a matter to Fénelon. He spared himself nothing in the attempt to help the young Burgundy fashion for himself a picture of a great and good ruler. Essentially the respect be-

tween the prince and his tutor was mutual, for both were set to
pursue an ideal of spiritual perfection. Years later, after the
death of the prince, Père Martineau asked Fénelon to give him
some recollections on the prince.

Cambrai, November 14, 1712.

I shall be only too glad if I can send you anything worthy of your
great subject . . . Of his childhood I can, at least, assure you that I
always found him open and sincere, so much so that one only needed to
ask him to discover his misdeed. One day he was in a very bad temper,
and in his anger desired to conceal that he had disobeyed. I urged him
to speak the truth before God. He fell into a great passion, exclaiming:
"Why do you ask me before God? As you have asked me thus I cannot
deny that I have done such-and-such a thing." He was beside himself
with anger, nevertheless religion had sufficient power to force a
humiliating confession from him. We never corrected him unless it
was absolutely necessary and then only with much discretion. As soon
as his excitement had passed he would come to whoever had rebuked
him, acknowledge his fault, make it up with that person, and bear no
ill-will afterwards. I have often known him to say, when he might
speak freely, "I am leaving the Duke of Burgundy outside the door,
with you I am only little Louis." [This was when he was nine years
old.]

Whenever he wished to talk on subjects that would instruct him,
I gave up lessons at once. This happened often. We came back to lessons
very easily, for he was fond of them, and I wished him to be fond of
sensible conversation also, to make him sociable and ready to get a
knowledge of people in society. The progress that he made during
these conversations in literary, political, and metaphysical subjects was
evident . . . By such treatment his temper grew sweeter; he became
gentle, good-natured, and merry; he delighted everyone . . . I have
never known him to care about praise . . . He has often told me
that he should remember the pleasure he took in uninterrupted study
all his life. He cared so much for the things he desired to learn that

I have known him to ask to be read to during meals and dressing. Moreover, I have never known a child so young listen to gems of poetry and oratory with such appreciation. He grasped the most abstract ideas with ease. If he saw me doing anything for him, he would set to work to do it in the same way, not waiting to be told to do so . . . He had a friendly regard for a certain number of worldly people whom he considered deserving of it, but he reserved his confidence for those who were honestly religious . . . I have never known anyone to whom one could tell the plainest of home truths with so little risk of offending; I have had extraordinary experience of this.

With years, and experience of things and people, and a position of authority, he acquired a strength in which he was somewhat lacking formerly. Constant occupation diverted him from trifling pleasures, and gave him a dignity of which his nature was always capable. If it seemed to him that the interests of religion, of justice, of honor, truth, or commercial integrity were concerned, he took his stand with a firmness that could not be assailed.

This letter tells as much about tutor as about pupil. How much ingenuity went into the bending of this royal twig! If the tree had not been prematurely cut down it might have sheltered a nation against the strong winds of adversity that were already blowing at the time of the death of Louis XIV.

It was with kingship in mind that Fénelon invented the epic known as *Télémaque*. For many generations of students, it would have been unnecessary to comment on this tale; everybody read it. At first, in the days when tales of adventure were rarer and mystery stories not yet a cult, everybody—young and old—read *Télémaque* for its own sake. Later, French students read it as literature and the English read it both as literature and as a means of acquiring good French. "*Calypso ne pouvait se consoler...* " these words were as familiar as *Gallia est omnis divisa . . ."* Many a nineteenth-century scholar has reported the verve with which *Télémaque* was read for the first time; and being required to memorize long passages did not destroy the charm of adventure. Today few, except students of the period, bother to read it in its entirety.

The tale starts with the arrival of Telemachus, son of Odysseus, on the island where Calypso still bewails her faithless lover. The young hero resists the allurements of an early and frivolous love and the enticements of Calypso to search for his father. His adventures with Mentor, who is actually the goddess Minerva disguised as a dignified and grave male counselor, in quest of the wanderer, his excursions into the tremendous adventures, fierce wars and great disasters of the kingdoms of tyrants and ideal rulers, are sown thickly with moral admonitions for the benefit of the pupil. The style is graceful and noble though lacking in forcefulness. There are passages of arbitrary realism, such as the description of the goddess as ravished by the pangs of unrequited love. In the description of the punishment of the unjust kings in Hades appears the vivid descriptive power of the author. One sees them chained and tormented by their subjects whom they had oppressed during their lifetime. Passages of a poetic tone are not uncommon, such as the description of the god of wine: "Bacchus too appeared crowned with ivy, leaning with one hand on his thyrsus and holding with the other an undulating vine branch, flowing with tendrils and studded with bunches of grapes. His was a mild beauty, with an indefinable something of

[87]

noble, of passionate and of melancholy; it was so that he appeared before the unhappy Ariadne when he found her alone, abandoned and sunk in grief, forlorn upon an unknown shore."

Again, in somewhat lighter mood, a rather pleasing fantasy is presented in the picture where "the great whales and all the monsters of the deep, letting forth and drawing in again the bitter waters in a continual flux and reflux, hastened forth out of their deep grottoes in their haste to see the goddess Calypso." It is of course in the pictures of kings, courts and states, both benevolent and depraved, that *Télémaque* has held its interest. It is these aspects of the book that helped bring about Fénelon's unhappy relationship with Louis XIV. Taking into account his ambitions and his fluid, subtle mind, it seems impossible that Fénelon should not have intended references to the king and to the court.

In its original purpose *Télémaque* was more than graceful sentiment and a guide for youthful royalty, cloaked in seductive if somewhat somniferous prose. In this tale based on the Odyssey and written ostensibly solely for the young Duke of Burgundy lies not too deep beneath the surface another of those fragments of dynamite that blew the French Revolution into flame. In *Télémaque* is foreseen Beaumarchais and Rousseau, as well as the Encyclopedists. In it unjust tyrants are held up for sharp analysis, but so—and most sympathetically—are those who rule with wisdom, affection for their people, and strict honor in all political dealings.

"Happy are the people who are ruled by a wise king. They live in happiness and plenty and look with love upon him to whom they owe their well-being. It is thus, Telemachus, that you should reign and compass the welfare of subjects if it shall please the gods to bring you into possession of your father's kingdom." A good king "is all-powerful over his people, but the laws are all-powerful over him. His power to do good is absolute. But his hands are bound when he would fain do ill." His life is not his own. "Not for himself did the gods make him king, but that he might give himself to his people . . . Authority by itself never did any good. It is not enough that the people should submit. We must win their hearts . . . All men are brothers and should love one another as brothers." War is both wicked and unprofitable even for the victor; all conquest is unjust. Freedom of trade is part of the foundation of good society. A man is rich, in a good society, not according to what he can accumulate but according to what he can do without. But Fénelon does not advocate that all men are equal just because they are brothers; there are seven ranks or classes, each with distinctive garb and duties. J. Lewis May, the Catholic biographer, has remarked that "in Fénelon's state . . . we have Liberté, within bounds; Fraternité; but not Egalité."

This was the book that most delighted the young prince. It was not published at the time it was written—1693 and 1694—although it is probable that many living at court became familiar with the adventures and the political philosophy of the book. Only after Fénelon had fallen into disfavor with the king was the book finally made public (1699), and then not by Fénelon himself. His enemies accused him, naturally, of making his unjust monarch a copy of Louis XIV, to which Fénelon makes the common-sense reply: "I wrote it when I was enjoying the many marks of confidence and generosity which the king had lavished upon me. I should surely have proved myself, not only the most ungrateful but the most foolish of men, had I taken occasion to draw an unflattering or ironic portrait of one to whom I was so indebted. It will be seen that I deal only in generalities. It is a story written at high speed and in detached fragments, and the whole stands in great need of revision." Certainly it achieved its immediate end: it instructed, entertained, and edified the prince for whom it was written.

At the same time Fénelon was directing his energies toward the education of the young prince, he was acting as spiritual counselor to an increasing number of men and women in high circles. His correspondence absorbed many hours of each busy week. Then, too, he continued as a scholar, taking part in the theological and philosophical controversies of his day. Nor were the controversies abstract dialectics: in them there was emotional involvement with living men and women. Conversation and argument, comment and retort—by such things his spirit was shaped.

5

Crosscurrents

FÉNELON's residence at court as preceptor to the Duke of
Burgundy covered the eight central years of his life and in
that span the most climactic episodes of his career were enacted.
Up to this period the course of his life had been an upward
swing with no regression and apparently still higher ascent was
assured. In time he could expect to wear a cardinal's hat. Had
this been his fortune it is possible that he would be of as
little significance to the religious world today as are his contemporary churchmen. The spiritual genius who does not attain
outward success is generally the voice that speaks beyond his
era—Jesus on the mountain, Paul from a Roman prison, Francis
barefoot on the road to Rome, Brother Lawrence from a kitchen.

Ambition was not absent from Fénelon's nature. Portraits
generally reveal a man of aristocratic and proud bearing—
although kindly—rather than a man unconcerned about him-

self or one easily submissive to the circumstances of life. His sensitivity to egotism in the men and women whom he counseled might indicate as well that this tendency to pride was also his own weakness. On the other hand, the fact of his noble birth and the ease with which he acquired a following among men and women of the court would have given him a justifiable expectation of promotion in the natural course of events. To a less favored man, such as Bossuet, whose attainment to higher favor depended on his personal genius and effort, advancement would depend upon ambition.

However, two factors made the central period of Fénelon's life rather than an easy ascent to further honor, instead a series of unhappy skirmishes ending in a decline of outward position. One factor was the state of the church, which was strained by the reactionary and revolutionary forces pulling her apart. The spirit of rationalism was abroad. This experimentation with truth and *methodical doubt* was pressing hard against the brittle crystallization that the church had made of its dogma. The period of French mysticism was coming to an end and the age of reason and atheism was at hand. The second factor was Fénelon's own nature, which would not let him speak entirely out of tradition. He could not give an answer out of a book, but spoke rather out of his own deep perception of truth—simply and naturally. Bossuet, on the other hand, remained a great churchman because he could give the conditioned reply to the questions of the age. The bishop of Meaux became known as a prodigy of equilibrium in a period that feared lack of balance. It was the age of the Golden Mean, the apotheosis of the established order.

Crosscurrents

In the seventeenth century four controversies occupied the
religious stage, and inevitably the political one as well. These
conflicts were contemporary, interwoven and changing in intensity to such a degree that no one of them can be considered
alone, and to understand Fénelon it is necessary to see him
against this background of turmoil. Huguenots against Catholics,
Gallicans against ultramontanes, and Jansenists against Jesuits
—these were the three prolonged ecclesiastical and political
wars of the period. A fourth was the quietism-mysticism quarrel
between Bossuet and Fénelon, of which Mme. Guyon's spiritual
difficulties were the precipitating incident. Of these controversies none has significance for the average man today except
the Fénelon-Bossuet affair, and then only because of the significance it had in the life of Fénelon. Through it he learned
the meaning of trouble and sorrow and henceforth was able
to speak to the troubled and sorrowing beyond his time.

From the time of Henry IV there had been in the church two
irreconcilable forces: on one extreme were adherents to the
church on a purely official basis, who observed its forms as long
as it was under civil authority; on the other extreme were the
ultramontanes represented by the Jesuits and the queens, Marie
de'Medici and Anne of Austria. From the official zealots
came Descartes, who in 1641 gave the world that reasonable
work *Meditations,* in which he offered proof of God, immortality, and freedom in rational terms but left to faith the nature
of God, the meaning of happiness, and the use of freedom.
He approached the borderline between philosophy and religion
and then stopped short. Cartesians in Paris fastened on reason
and let go of faith, making a philosophical sect that seized upon

[93]

the least profitable of their mentor's doctrines and did not continue his method of searching. The cool reasoning of the Cartesians scorned the blind devotion of Italian piety and the torrid ecstasies of Spanish mysticism that were also a part of the Catholic picture. St. Evremond said that rational religion could not be found in either Italy or Spain, but that thanks to Gallican liberties it might be saved in France if it left behind the girdle of St. Margaret and took to reading Bossuet.

The Gallican liberties had never been officially given to France but had grown up in the very nature of things, and assured the rights of Frenchmen against the domination of the Roman See. From the Sorbonne its advocates carried on a theological warfare with the Jesuit colleges. The whole struggle to maintain Gallican liberties in French Catholicism is interwoven with violent intervention on the part of the Jesuits, who had sworn to uphold Holy Church. In spite of their activities, Richelieu had been able successfully to hold to his purpose to unify France and extend the king's power, a task that Louis XIV carried on with zest. In the "Declaration of the Four Articles" he strengthened his control over the church although he himself was becoming more and more devoted to the observances of his mother's religion. Mme. de Maintenon continued to further the king's religious inclinations and was hopeful that he would eventually manifest the virtues of true spirituality. Her hope was obviously never fulfilled. On one occasion she wrote to Cardinal de Noailles that, although the king never missed a fast day, he did not know the meaning of humility.

For Bossuet Gallicanism meant not only the divine right of kings, but the divine establishment of sovereignty whether monarchical or republican. No power on earth could interfere with the system or the lawfully appointed officers, whether they were bad or good, nor could one form be exchanged for another. Political stability at all costs was the essential basis of Bossuet's policy, for he remembered too clearly the low state of France during the Fronde warfare. His was the high accomplishment of reconciliation between the pope and Louis XIV in the Gallican-Ultramontane crisis of 1682-1693 and by his statesmanship on this occasion he became the dominant figure in the church for more than twenty years. He worked to preserve the sacredness of the Gallican liberties and to release the king from the pope's jurisdiction while at the same time giving the right of judgment to the pope and the bishops jointly. By his temporizing in this final conflict of the Gallicans he reconciled faith and reason in the church and brought many freethinkers into the fold.

Satire and cynicism were prevalent among the intellectuals outside the church. Boredom, sophistication and disillusionment were apparent on all sides. The deists had separated the world from its Creator and set it spinning along its way with no other salvation than a code of infallible laws. Man did what he could with it. Higher criticism, with its eternal questioning, had been born in the Oratory. Richard Simon, father of modern German exegesis, had already published his scandalizing and ruthless translations of the Bible, transgressing beyond the heretical fields explored by Père Dupin, an ancient theological enemy of Bossuet's. Fénelon remarked in one of his letters of this period: "I was delighted to see the vigor of the old doctor and the old bishop. I pictured you to myself, skullcap pulled over your ears, holding M. Dupin like an eagle seizing in its claws a feeble sparrow hawk."

Bayle, that literary journalist and spokesman of skepticism, with his passion for learning and reason, was attacking the prejudices of all common people, Catholic and Huguenot alike. He maintained that a society of honest atheists was better than a society of idolaters. He was a Cartesian to a degree, setting forth that there was in every man an innate morality independent of the moral dogma of his environment. For him, however, there was no supernatural and eternal purpose for being. "Without God," said his adversaries, "morality is meaningless." Needless to say, such daring liberalism brought consternation to upholders of the faith and called forth a sharp edict from Versailles, forbidding all persons other than professors by title to lecture publicly on canonical or civil laws. This edict was later expanded to ban the assembling of students in any faculty member's house.

The philosophy of John Locke, with its utilitarian ethic, had by 1700 been translated and had found a growing edge among the freethinkers. This group became a rallying point for all who were impatient with dogmatism wherever it existed, whether among Cartesians or Jesuit ecclesiastics. The university and the Jesuits were combined against the Cartesians, and Oratorians were forbidden to teach the philosophy of the famous Parisian. However, books on philosophy could not be suppressed and St. Regis set himself to spread the teaching of Descartes. He wrote prolifically, commenting upon his compatriot without seriously applying his method—creating something of a philosophical fad rather than inspiring to philosophical search. Spinoza's mind was inaccessible to the average French mind of the day and only a few gave him attention, while among religious philosophers he stirred up an emotional terror. Freethinkers were curious about him and religious thinkers considered him an *unbeliever*. It was, says Henri Martin, a hundred and fifty years before his influence was manifest in France.

Freethinkers, however, did not disturb Bossuet so much as the indifference to religion and the apathy of the time that disguised itself in a mad pursuit of business or pleasure. Rational indifference appalled not only the bishop of Meaux but even the skeptics themselves. La Bruyère wrote: "Atheism does not exist. The high personages who are most suspected of it are too lazy to make up their minds that God does not exist; their indolence extends to the point of making them cold and listless about this matter. . . . Just as it does about the nature of their souls and the deductions to be drawn from true religion."

Fénelon expressed to the Duc d'Orléans his own anxiety about this prevailing mental indolence that did not question anything. "We come into this world all of a sudden, as fallen from the skies; we neither know what we are, nor whence we came, nor whither we are come, nor with whom we live, nor where we shall go upon our departure from here. . . . Nobody cares to unravel the mystery, we amuse ourselves with everything. We want to know all things but the only one which above all things concerns us. This monstrous laziness is the sin of unbelief. . . . Men take it for granted that God is because they dare not examine themselves. An indifference that grows out of their passions for other objects possesses them. They know God as something mysterious, unintelligible and far removed, a powerful, austere being. . . . All that a real philosopher needs, beyond a due conviction of his ignorance, is anxiety to discover what he is, and astonishment that, as yet, he does not know it."

So in seventeenth-century France, with its conformity, orthodoxy, and classical compromise, its boredom and rebellion, the soil was becoming fertile for the ideas of the eighteenth century. It was a time in which the old had been lived out and the new was not yet born, a time of reaction and revolution. Pascal personifies the hesitation of the period as he "searches lamenting." The mysteries, doubts, and contradictions of his soul were not characteristic of the spiritual stalwarts of the preceding era such as Vincent de Paul, Cardinal Bérulle, St. John of the Cross, Ignatius Loyola; or outside of the old church the virile Protestants: Martin Luther, John Calvin, George Fox—all of whom helped to reshape the picture of Western Christianity. The former era in Western Europe had been marked by a courageous faith and a vigorous evangelism.

Pascal was early identified with the Jansenists, the century-old enemies of the Jesuits. The Jansenists represent the first vocal reaction against the Jesuit formal methods of education and spiritual training of the will. They maintained that religion did not consist in believing a particular doctrine or in adopting a mode of life; rather, it depended entirely on a *conversion* experience. In Blaise Pascal's *Memorial* is recorded the ecstasy for which the Jansenists were waiting in their convent at Port-Royal and which many claimed to have experienced. In its few phrases he recaptured the *certitude and joy* of the Divine Union. An overwhelming revelation of God was essential to salvation, but only God himself could choose to reveal himself.

Morality and orthodoxy, creeds and offices are, the Jansenists said, appropriate and necessary but they are never to be mistaken for means to salvation. They can have meaning only after the conversion experience, otherwise they are hypocritical actions. Everything hangs on the action of the Divine Will, which can descend like a whirlwind when it chooses and sweep one man into the stillness of its inmost heart and leave another in the outer chaos. When God chooses the soul is brought irresistibly, unfailingly, victoriously out of darkness into light.

Jansenius drew his tenets from St. Augustine. The will of man is, he stated, the victim of the inimical dualism of his nature; flesh is evil and spirit is good and the human will lies helpless between the two attractions as a bit of filing between two magnets.

The arbitrary God of the Jansenists did not appall the great numbers of men and women who centered around Port-Royal and the larger numbers of followers who eagerly received their doctrine. In the average mind of that day there was no particular repugnance to a God conceived of in terms of an absolute monarch. The Jansenists were simply transferring their loyalty to a superior ruler, a sufficient reason for the hatred and uneasiness of Louis XIV and the Jesuits. The grimness of predestination was softened by the fact that God's will was flexible and that while on one day a man might be unregenerate the next day it might please God to choose him. Therefore the only way left for any man was to search lamenting. The appeal of Jansenism to the more liberal minds of France was its freedom from form. Many religious seekers of the period were weary of the formality of the Jesuit system with its confidence in techniques. The Ignatian system was a thorough and unsparing organization of the spiritual life which presented a definite barrier to the spontaneous spiritual person. It was a system by which the human will was disciplined until it could unflinchingly obey the direction of the "general." One remembers that Loyola had been a soldier lamed in battle. What the Jansenists were trying to say was: men cannot make their own religion, they can neither experiment with a rationally conceived God nor can they depend on holy trinkets from Rome. A preconceived end acquired by a formula of imagination, intellect, and will is useless. Man must be content to wait until God moves in his direction.

On the other hand, Ignatius of Loyola had devised the *Spiritual Exercises* for the Society of Jesus so that its members might become valiant soldiers of the church. His rules were not primarily a means to Christian perfection, although perfection of personality was a station en route to the larger end of doing the work of Providence. They proposed to transform the individual from self-centeredness to God-centeredness by the work of his own will in co-operation with the grace of God. Every man ended his meditation with a resolution and made an active choice of direction. "The end of the Spiritual Exercises," says Father Rickeby, "is such amount and quality of self-denial as shall bring you to do the work given you by obedience or by Providence wholly, steadily, intelligently, courageously, cheerfully." The meditation of the Jesuit teaching did not exclude the deeper levels of prayer as Père Lallemont explains: "To meditate upon hell is to see a painted representation of a lion; whilst by contemplation upon hell, the living lion stands before you." Ignatius warned against overintellectualizing and overstaying in the *Exercises*. "It is not the abundance of knowledge that fills and satisfies the soul, but the inward sense and taste of things." When the inward taste of things, its life and meaning, has escaped from the system, then the system becomes unlovely and vicious, and the more unlovely and vicious the system the more insistent and violent are its advocates.

Although Fénelon was nearer to the Jansenists in their fluidity of spirit than he was to the Jesuits, he differed so fundamentally from them on the matter of free will that in the conflict he necessarily was on the side of the Jesuits. His teachings always expressed the reciprocal relationship between God and man, the meeting in which man necessarily wills to participate. With him there was implicit in his being the power to choose. Or, there is "an obligation of mutual understanding," as Baron von Hügel said, in all the changes that transpire in the human soul as it becomes more and more purified. Human nature chooses in the end to be responsive to the supernatural

François de Fénelon

grace of God. "Our will is but a reflection of his own, he works immediately in us, an indistinguishable partner when *we choose.* Our choice is His and ours alike."

The character of French Catholicism had been affected not only by the rational tendencies of the times and the Jesuits' spiritual exercises, but also by elaborate ceremonies and a superstitious regard for the objects of worship, as well as "bad little books of devotion" that had come from Italy and out of which had sprung quietistic extravagances among the mystically inclined.

While the intellectually gifted were venturing out into the rare atmosphere between philosophy and religion, the simple-minded were seeking security by an extraordinary devotion to the ceremonies of the church. Between these were those who were finding meaning in the symbols and who by means of them were being led to the spiritual plains of the soul. In a letter to the Duc d'Orléans Fénelon offers his conception of the use of ceremony:

"Ceremonies are instituted not as being the essential part of religion but only to serve as signs which show it and nourish it in itself and help to communicate it to others. Those ceremonies are in respect to God what the tokens of respect are to a father whom his children salute, embrace, and serve with earnestness. . . . As soon as the internal worship is admitted the external is requisite to express it and communicate it to society. They are a means of recollection."

There is an aspiring, spiritual splendor in the Gothic cathedrals and the ritual of the church at all times. We are indebted to Benoît de Canfield for a description of the services of the day as well as for the reaction such external glory had

[102]

upon a priest accustomed to the colder, more reserved atmosphere of the England from which he had lately come. They filled him with awe and seemed to transport him to Paradise itself. "When I beheld the lofty and magnificent buildings of thy temple [his remarks are directed to the Deity] the great and spacious monasteries, beautiful within and without, with sculpture, paintings and exquisite carvings, I could think of nothing but the gravity and majesty of thy holy Church . . . beholding the great solemnity of the Mass, celebrated by priests, deacons, subdeacons, acolytes, each with the ornaments of his rank and each performing his own office; beholding the dressed altar glittering with candles and encircled by the choir; beholding the devotion and piety with which they censed it with goodly fragrance and the great and solemn processions of thronging worshipers and torches, candles and numberless tapers; the choir filled with priests, clerks and choristers in white . . . the ineffable melodies, the incomparable and divine harmony of well-tuned organs and the sweet voices which sang together . . . celestial things flowed into my heart."

From Spain there flowed into French Catholicism the ardor of mystics, and new religious orders flourished. Monasteries and convents were innumerable, some of them luxurious and most worldly havens for the nobility and others austere shelters for ascetics and mystics. Bremond reports that "monasteries viewed from afar give the clearest impression of laxity, yet with the saints groaning in the dark agonizing for reform."

The period of post-Renaissance mysticism was late in France. It had followed soon upon the Renaissance in Germany, Spain, and England and had reshaped religion with its fresh and spontaneous experiences as well as manifested the dangers of uncontrolled ecstasy. Behind the French mystics there lay the whole body of mystical theology from the time of Clement downward. Evelyn Underhill points out that the tendency of the French mystics to place the whole of religion in an unconditioned self-yielding to God accounted for its quietistic emphasis. It was, she says, "a noble error"—the shadowy side of that turning of the religious consciousness toward pure adoration and away from self-consideration. On the other hand, this drift to passivity was checked by the inflow of Teresian mysticism that carried with it a concrete, active manifestation of the spiritual intake. While, on the one hand, the end of the century was marked by its quietistic tendencies it was also notable, on the other, for the extreme activity of its mystics. Seventeenth-century France was full of mystics of all kinds and temperaments, in the cloister and out of it. And to this company belongs François de Fénelon.

The line begins with Benoît de Canfield and extends through Mme. Acarie, Cardinal Bérulle, Vincent de Paul, Brother Lawrence, François de Sales, Jeanne de Chantal, Mme. Guyon, and Fénelon. Not only were these men and women active in the religious orders of their day but they were also focal points around which revolved small groups devoted to intensive training in what had become almost an art of the spirit. Mme. Acarie, a widow with six children, carried on her husband's business, counseled hundreds of Parisians, visited convents constantly, and at the same time was the inspiration of many significant spiritual movements of her day. It was Mme. Acarie who urged

Pierre Bérulle to establish the French Oratory; it was she who
was responsible for bringing to France the Spanish nuns, which
furthered reform among all orders; it was Mme. Acarie who
gave to François de Sales the inspiration to become the authority
he was on the direction of souls.

Benoît de Canfield gave the century its first book of instruction on the spiritual life and in it can be traced all that went
before and a shadow of all that the succeeding works of
France's notable mystics have given the world. William Fitch,
later Benoît de Canfield, wandered in Franciscan fashion from
an Essex village. He was sixty years old when he came to Paris,
where for twenty years he taught his *Règle de Perfection*—a
Capuchin friar who, Bremond says, outdistanced them all by
the splendor of his mystic genius and the extent of his influence.
On the cover of his little handbook he had made a beautiful
diagram portraying the three stages of the mystical life. It
was an image of the sun filled with faces placed in three con-
centric circles; the faces on the outer rim are scarcely visible in
the darkness and are surrounded by very earthy tools, upon
which light falls at different points; the faces in the second
row are more clearly illumined by the light of the sun, they
have laid the tools aside; the third row of faces is almost lost
in the light itself. The Sun is the Will of God and the three
rows represent degrees of commitment to that Will. The faces
in the first row show the actives whose work is caught up in the
light of God, the second row the contemplatives who have laid
aside their active works, and the inner circle those who have
attained union with God.

The author explains: "This image shows us that despite the

twilight encompassing it, the humble active life of the beginner is not opposed to the contemplative quietude of the perfect. The better a soul fulfills the duties of her station, the nearer she approaches the sun . . . Let us beware of despising these tools, or the rudimentary works of our powers, but let us not be satisfied. Let us not be misled by fears or vanity, on the other hand, and refuse to mount higher. Otherwise we fall into the error of those who, too much given to the ministry of Martha, refuse to choose with Mary the better part."

The *Rule* continues: "To remedy this error and reduce these superfluous acts, know that interior life is not perfected nor is true contemplation acquired by discourses, which are acts of the will: for by no intellectual speculation can God be possessed or enjoyed, but solely by the love of Him . . . For intellectual speculation would fain adopt God, the All-Powerful, Infinite, Incomprehensible, to our petty capacity; while the will, on the contrary, acting by love, seeks to adapt itself in some degree to the infinity and almightiness of God . . . Such intellectual speculation is a human thing, causing us to dwell in ourselves, but the will of God is a Divine thing, raising and drawing us out of ourselves, transforming us into the Divine . . . in these changeless depths the Spirit approaches so close to the soul that she perceives His very shadow."

Whether Canfield was familiar with the *Cloud of Unknowing,* the work of an anonymous countryman of his, is not evident, but both use the language of Dionysius, both are working through the language of darkness and light, and both distrust the intellect. "Love may reach to God in this life, but not knowing . . . I would leave all that thing that I can think, and choose to love that thing I cannot think. For he may well be loved but not thought. By love he may be gotten and holden; but by thought never. . . . Let God draw thy love up to that cloud; and strive thou through help of his grace to forget all other things."

It is useless to attempt a definition of mysticism, for like all deep experience it defies definition. Just as love and reverence cannot be defined nor the meaning conveyed to those who have not had a like experience, the direct knowledge of the Divine is incommunicable. Yet he who has loved and reverenced by the very nature of his experiences never gives up trying to translate them into understandable terms—by gentleness of spirit, by symbolism of music, words or color—for only so does the experience become real. . . . This effort to make the experience live for others is a test of its validity, gives it meaning. To the inexperienced in love and reverence there is always given a latent potentiality for such an experience, therefore he asks, "How can I come to know?" Then it is that the experienced one seeks to devise a method in hope of reproducing the climate in which love and reverence may be felt. But the method does not infallibly produce the experience because that which is sought after is the formless and cannot be captured at will by the formal. So appears the pattern and problem of mystics from time immemorial.

There seems to be a divine purpose for the mystical experience —to bring into the world of things the invisible wisdom by which the visible may be given its significance. The full mystical experience consists in the double movement of getting and giving—it is a dyastole-systole rhythm. If the experience is a full one it results in a transmutation of personality in the individual and an enlarged consciousness whereby he perceives not only his vertical relationship with God but his horizontal relationship with his fellows—and even with a lower form of being, as is evidenced in the symbiosis that is apparent between saints and the animal world. A sort of receptive consciousness seems to accompany the mystical experience. The mystic feels himself at one with God. Eternity enters into him . . . he is penetrated and momentarily transformed into the heart of all being, the center of existence. Even the mountain may become Buddha. So comes the inbreathing experience of the Infinite Presence.

Evelyn Underhill, in her comprehensive study *Mysticism,* draws a definite distinction between mystical philosophers and "true" mystics; only those who have lived the life are worthy to be so named, she says. Those who share in the mystical experience include the lover, the mourner, the poet. They have all lifted for a moment the veil of Isis. The act of contemplation is a psychic gateway, a means of going from one state of consciousness to another; the field of perception is shifted. The mystics in general agree that in the final stage of the soul's progress, to accomplish the ultimate "death to itself," it is, as it were, cast into a crucible. When it emerges it has been crushed and is changed, so that it is entirely other.

St. Teresa proposed for her nuns a test as to the healthiness of their mystical experiences. She said they must bear witness.

in the world of outer relationship. "Our Lord asks but two things of us: love of him and for our neighbor; but this is what we must strive to obtain. . . . I think the most certain sign that we keep these two commandments is that we have a genuine love for others. We cannot know whether we love God, although there may be strong reasons for thinking so, but there can be no doubt about whether we love our neighbor."

The method used by the saints—contemplation—and the results of such a practice are not necessarily holy. The history of mystical movements in all religions has revealed a line of partial mysticism—a sort of montanistic movement. Its devotees have cultivated ecstatic phenomena, either consciously or unconsciously, for the sake of the experience, and not to realize the unfolding purpose of the Eternal. Altruism does not emanate from such groups; instead, there has been an exaltation of the ego as an agent of something beyond the grasp of the ordinary man or woman. Occultism, illuminism, and other perversions of the mystical powers are dangerous and confusing. Whenever mysticism rises in a society, the two streams are in evidence— the partial and the complete go hand in hand. Beside St. John and the Neoplatonists were the Gnostics; beside Eckhart and Ruysbroeck were the Brethren of the Free Spirit, the Rosecrucians and other anarchical groups; beside St. John of the Cross and St. Teresa were the Illuminati; and in the highest period of French mysticism a similar illuminism broke out.

Each mystical age repeats the experience gained by its spiritual forebears, even while each gives its own peculiar emphasis to the fundamental Truth so discovered. Christian mysticism arose in apostolic days with St. John; indeed, the mystical experience was taken for granted, says Dom John Chapman in his long discussion of mysticism in *Hastings Encyclopedia of Religion and Ethics.* Clement, following St. John and St. Paul, insists that the contemplation of God is the goal of Christian achievement, and suggests the three levels of progress toward this goal—purification, enlightenment, and union. In the fourth century asceticism and discipline were deliberately assumed as a means to the mystical experience through an adaptation of the Greek mysteries into Christian practice. Cassian, about A.D. 350, developed the idea that the life of communion with God ascends by gradual steps that keep pace with the self's increasing purification until it reaches a state of pure adoration. "Lifted up with fervor of heart to a certain burning prayer which the speech of man cannot express, nor the thought of man comprehend it attains at last a more sublime and exalted condition which is brought about by the contemplation of God alone and by ardent love; wherein the mind, as though it were flung and dissolved into his love converses with him in utmost familiarity . . . but in the end when we are lifted up and established in this sublime state, as children of God, we shall be no longer concerned with our own selfish interests, we shall seek solely in all *things* the honor and glory of our Father."

It was through Augustine, bishop of Hippo, that Plotinus entered the stream, and ever since then mystics have found him a companion of the way. Augustine in early life loved, sinned, and endured temptation. He was a self-centered intellectual with an attractive personality until "By inward goads Thou didst rouse me, that I should be ill at ease until Thou wert manifested to my inward sight . . . Thou wert more inward to me than my most inward part. I awoke in Thee and saw Thee infinite and this sight was not derived from flesh . . . God speaks to man, not by means of some audible creature dinning in his ears . . . nor by means of a spiritual being with the semblance of a body . . . he speaks by the Truth itself, if any one is prepared to hear with the mind rather than with the body. He speaks to that part of man which is better than all else in him, and than which God himself is better." Sometimes it is the heart, sometimes the will and sometimes the mind by which he finds God, but however "our whole work in this life is to heal the eyes of the heart by which we see God." However, he stresses the work of the will in this movement Godward. He refers to the "momentous will"—"Thither one journeys not in ships, nor in chariots, nor on foot; for to journey thither, nay even to arrive there is nothing else but the will to go . . . To will God entirely is to have Him!"

This experience is *nous*—knowledge in which the whole being participates, an actual realization of the wholeness of beauty, truth, and goodness within and without one's self. He himself becomes "a sponge filled from the unmeasured sea of God." He foreshadows Dionysius in his manner of conceiving of God as beyond all that appears. "God is best adored in silence; best known by nescience; best described by negatives."

However, vision of God is not the goal of his mystical striving. The highest state is one of *union*—"I heard as the heart heareth Thy voice, 'I am the food of them that are full grown;

[111]

grow and thou shalt feed on Me, nor shalt thou transmute Me into thee . . . but thou shalt be transmuted into me.' "

Following Augustine in the fifth century, although not translated until the ninth century, was Dionysius the Areopagite, who exercised the greatest influence of all on medieval mystics and provided the conceptions of Ruysbroeck and Eckhart. He brought into Christian mysticism an awe-struck sense of the unsearchable divine transcendence, "the divine darkness . . . the light unapproachable . . . a deep but dazzling darkness." Above all that originates is the "super-original Origin . . . the uncreated One, who stands back of his creation and from whom all things flow and into which all things must return." Divine love is "an eternal circle from goodness through goodness to goodness." The soul of man has two parts and with the higher he has potentiality of seeing by divine reflection but with the lower he perceives only by symbols. Both the lower and the higher part of the soul cannot act at the same time, therefore to return to God the soul leaves all its faculties which use symbols, strips off all that is not pure essence and "just as those who make a lifelike statue chip off all the encumbrance, cut away the superfluous material and bring to light the Beauty hidden within, so we negate everything in order that without veils we may know the Unknown which is concealed by all the light of existing things." Hence Neoplatonism was welded into the mystical stream.

Meister Eckhart followed close upon Dionysius in his thinking. He lived at a time when heretical mysticism was at its height in Germany and was able to push his speculations "beyond the flaming bounds of time and space" even while he kept contact with the common people who flocked to him by the thousands to listen to his simple sermons preached in the vernacular. He was able to do this by positing the Godhead as the "Wordless One" and God as the "Uttered Word." He revived the sense of awe that is fundamental to a comprehension of spiritual truth while at the same time formulating what is equally necessary, a personal, ever-loving, present God who is in the Eternal Now of all existence. In this very beholding of Himself there comes into being the idea of the universe. "In the Godhead there is no number for He is One, but in time and space there are divisions—parts. If my face were eternal, and I held it before a time-mirror, it would be received by the mirror in time, yet it would itself be eternal." This same unnatured nature is the essence and ground of the soul of man by which he is able to touch the Godhead once he ceases to identify himself with the lower part of his soul. It is the "Inmost Man . . . spark of the soul . . . *syntersis* . . . active reason."

Fénelon has said that it is the grandeur of the soul rooted deep, *a priori* in the bottom of the soul, "It is an unchangeable and universal law of righteousness by which all thought is corrected. It is fixed, immutable so internally rooted that I am tempted to take it for myself, where as it is far above me, corrects me, redresses me, puts me on guard against myself and warns me of my weakness . . . it inspires and preserves me incessantly. This internal rule is no other than my reason. But I speak of it without penetrating the force of the term . . . It

[113]

is myself and I must enter into myself to find it. But this superior reason is not mine. The rule is perfect and immutable, I am changeable and imperfect and when I go wrong this reason does not lose its integrity. This master is everywhere and his voice is heard from one end of the universe to the other, by all mankind as well as me . . . It is by this that men in all climates and all ages have been bound together to a certain immovable Center which holds them united by certain invariables, notwithstanding the infinite variety of opinions which may arise from human passions and caprices."

Three contemporaries of Meister Eckhart were Johann Tauler, Heinrich Suso, and Jan Ruysbroeck, all of whom were nurtured among the Friends of God, a community of spiritual seekers. Although many fanatical sects were springing up in Germany at the time and clairvoyance, prophecy, and abnormal phenomena were common experiences, the Friends of God through the stabilizing influence of Johann Tauler were able to maintain connection with the church and represent the best spiritual thought of the period. Out of this group came two of the world's most highly valued devotional classics, *Theologia Germanica* and the *Imitation of Christ*. There was in these three mystics that *liesse*—gladness with vigor—that drew thousands of men and women to them. Perhaps no healthier mysticism is spoken anywhere than that of Johann Tauler. Ruysbroeck and Tauler arrived at a state of mystical awareness through contemplation, whereas Suso practiced an asceticism that exceeds any described by other mystics, yet all of them manifest a similar result. With them unitive knowledge of God resulted in an "inward jubilee . . . a joy no tongue can tell, but which pours itself out with might through heart and soul."

Evelyn Underhill classes Jan Ruysbroeck as the greatest mystic of the church, for unlike the others he seems not to have undergone any spiritual crisis and to have made a steady ascent to the ineffable heights. His is an experience of *being* rather than of attaining a goal. His descriptive words are words of fullness rather than of emptiness: "All we taste, against all we lack, is like a single drop of water against the whole sea . . . for we feed upon His immensity which we cannot devour, and we yearn for His infinity which we cannot attain." He became a reformer of the false mysticism that was arising in Germany and spoke against spiritual indulgence just as strongly as against physical indulgence. Before those who would contemplate God only, he placed the ideal of Christ as a rule and pattern of living. For him there was no inconsistency between the *Imitation of Christ* and the *Via Negativa*. Christ is an active manifestation of God in the world and a genuine part of the mystical experience. His conception of Christ is similar to that of Augustine: "I am come as a Word from the heart, as a ray from the sun, as heat from the fire, as fragrance from the flower, as a stream from a perennial fountain." The generation of Christ is a continual process, the goodness of the Godhead that needs must impart itself forever.

Fénelon, too, holds this opinion of Christ. "Exiled here below during a moment infinitely short, Jesus Christ teaches us to regard this life as the infancy of our being and as an obscure night, of which all the pleasures are but fleeting dreams and evils salutary disgusts, to cause us to tend to our true country

. . . Penetrated with our nothingness, our helplessness, he teaches us to open our hearts without ceasing before the Being of beings, that he may retrace in us his image; he may embellish us with his beauty, enlighten and animate us; that he may give us well-being as well as being; reason as well as life, our perfect loves as our truer lights; that he may thus produce in us all the virtues, human and divine, till being conformed to himself, he can absorb and consummate us in his Divine unity."

It was at this juncture of the stream of mysticism that Benoît de Canfield lived and poured forth his experience and knowledge into French thinking. If Fénelon could have joined the mystical tradition at this point his experience would have been more easily incorporated into the stream. Bremond has observed that, had this been Fénelon's period, the *Maximes des Saintes* would not have been necessary and he might have written *Traité de l'Amour de Dieu,* François de Sales' classic contribution to Christian mystical theology. Between Canfield and Fénelon, however, the stream flowed through hearts of men and women who suffered through the Inquisition, and who were fired with a consuming desire to transcend earthy passions and fulfill the true purpose of their being; it was to pick up a system of theology and a method, it was to lose its pantheistic tendencies in the individualism of the Spanish character. Between Canfield and Fénelon were Ignatius of Loyola, St. John of the Cross, St. Teresa of Ávila, and St. François de Sales—each of whom put the unique stamp of his personality and age upon it.

6

Fire and Snow

AFTER the Spanish were driven by the Moslem invaders into the small mountainous section of the north, eight centuries passed before the land was entirely reconquered. During those centuries of struggle the Iberians absorbed much of the art and science of their conquerors, but a spirit of unyielding resistance burned continually in the hearts of the fragment of national life that remained. The fervor of the watchword "Conquer for the Cross" flamed before the eyes of those who had withdrawn to their northern fastnesses, whence they steadily pushed southward, year after year, century after century, until in the fifteenth century the Catholic monarchs Ferdinand and Isabella rode in triumph into Granada. Added to the natural disposition of the Spaniards, who were always intolerant of their foes and prone to violence and excess, this eight hundred years of devotion to an ideal developed in them a special character. Their inheritance is revealed in the fanatical intensity of their religious zeal, the cruelties of the Inquisition, the prodigies of will power developed by the early Jesuit missionaries, the remarkable accomplishments of the mystics.

The national life continued, a powerful, swiftly running stream, diving underground when necessary, emerging in exuberant and fantastic waves of art, genius, heroism, and hysteria. One sees the blend of traits amalgamating, the combination of violence and mysticism developed in a climate of ferocious extremes, blinding snows and parching suns, and complicated by widespread poverty. Thus flowed the stream of white light toward France and Fénelon. The writings of Eckhart, Tauler, Suso, and Ruysbroeck all entered Spain, only to be banished except for the last, whose symbolism and "fullness" of divine vision spoke more clearly to Spanish temperaments—for Spanish minds abhor abstractions. The Spanish spiritual seekers followed the classifications and language of medieval mystics, but they were more earthy in their expression of it. The truly great among them remained Orthodox Romanist—reforming from within. They observed the offices and ceremonies of the church meticulously. Whatever concerned them spiritually was given elaborate expression. One of the founders of the cathedral of Seville expresses it well: "Let us build so magnificent a temple that in ages to come men shall think us to be mad." So the "quiet rest" of St. Teresa and St. John of the Cross was not the "nothingness" of Dionysius and Eckhart, but a *rest most busy.*

Allison Peers refers to sixteenth-century Spain as the Golden Age of religion in which the mystical writings alone can be numbered by the thousands. Three great personalities colored mystical theology and practice for all time: Ignatius of Loyola, St. Teresa of Avila, and St. John of the Cross. These represent the three powers of the Counter reformation in Spain. All three were vigorous and passionate in their chosen vocation, and each imbibed a heritage of fierce devotion from Spain's sturdy defenders of the cross.

"The soul must be virile, not like those soldiers who lie down on their stomachs to drink . . . manna does not fall in the first habitations, we must press on if we want to gather it," counsels St. Teresa; and Arozco adds, "He who would see the face of the most powerful Wrestler, our boundless God, must first have wrestled with himself." St. John of the Cross is no less vigorous. "Strive to choose, not that which is easiest, but that which is most difficult . . . do not deprive your soul of the agility which it needs to mount up to Him." Teresa presses forward with zeal from mansion to mansion, while John, her companion in the way, as a pilgrim of the Dark Night of the Soul descends his staircase, leaves the house of himself in the dead of night and journeys to his goal. Both were energetic mystics.

Teresa was a comely woman of middle years when, in 1568, she first met John, the young Carmelite monk to whom she became an elder and venerated sister. "Why, thou art but half a friar," was her comment when she first saw him. But she soon discovered that the new recruit was more than an ordinary man in spite of his small stature and fragile body. Contrary to the usual opinion of this outstanding contemplative, he was not an aesthete living in the shelter of a cloister dreaming out poetry in the dim feeble light of his cell. From the time he was twelve years of age he labored with his hands: carpenter, tailor, wood carver, painter. Soon after he met Teresa he went with two companions to live in the miserable shelter that they called the "second Bethlehem," both to hold it for a new house of the Carmelites and to prepare it for occupancy.

The three friars did not scorn hard work in establishing these houses. They set themselves a schedule: they rose at four in the morning—matins, lauds, prime, mental prayer, and masses—then came a long day of pastoral work among the desperately poor; fatigued and hungry they returned to their miserable shelter for vespers, prayer, and a few hours of sleep. They, and indeed all who worked with Teresa, took on her simple, straightforward and dauntless spirit. Her down-to-earth courage blazes out in her accounts of founding the new houses of the Order. Fifteen are credited to her and St. John of the Cross.

"At Toledo we were for some days with no furniture but two straw mattresses and one blanket, not even a withered leaf to fry a sardine with, till someone, I know not who, moved by our Lord, put a faggot in the church with which we helped ourselves. At night it was cold, and we felt it . . . The poverty we were in seemed to me as the source of sweet contemplation . . . God gave me great courage, and the more grievous the trials the greater the courage, without weariness in suffering." The reformers stirred up a tumult in the relaxed Carmelite orders and the shadow of the Inquisition consequently fell upon them. Teresa was summoned and reprimanded many

times. And John, slandered and vilified, spent nine months in
the black hole of the jail at Toledo. While there he not only
composed exquisite poetry concerning the escape of his soul
from its bodily prison but actually contrived the escape of his
body from the prison. He did not wait to convert his jailers
as did St. Paul, but sped away to the welcoming shelter of
the Discalced Carmelites. Pain and peril nourished the poetry
of John and brought to his prose the validity of one who had
experienced suffering.

In the poetry of St. John of the Cross liquid syllables and
marvelous imagery shine through the lines and emit the white
light of the poet's purity. His philosophy is the blazing, difficult wisdom that finds the flame of love in the darkness beyond
itself. His great work is the *Dark Night of the Soul*.

> En una noche escura
> Con aesias en amores inflamada—

The music penetrates the veil of language.

> Upon an obscure night
> Fevered with Love's anxiety
> (O hapless, happy plight!)
> I went, none seeing me,
> Forth from my house, where all things quiet be

The *Dark Night of the Soul* was also a call to self-forgetting,
to stripping off all selfhood and unlikeness to God. John of
the Cross with Jan Ruysbroeck found emptiness to be the fullness of God. "I die because I do not die," he cries.

François de Fénelon

This life that has been giv'n to me
Is but true life's negation—nay,
'Tis death that comes with each new day
Until I live, my God, with Thee.

In this ideal of renunciation John of the Cross is as Spanish as he is Catholic, says Bede Frost. To the Spaniard death is essentially "life-giving" as can be seen in the songs of Iberian poets. It is life, not death, that triumphs in Spanish literature, art, and religion—and in the way they celebrate Good Friday. There is a consciousness of the exuberance of life victorious, blazing through the broken body of the Crucified around which rise the triumphal strains of the *Pange Lingua Gloriosa*. Behind the dazzling darkness is the flame of love that forever gives meaning to life in heaven and earth. Contemplation to them is the secret, peaceful, and loving influence of God shining through the heavy substance of the universe. It is God communicating through the soul as light through the window, or coal through the fire. "This communication of God diffuses itself substantially in the whole soul, or rather the soul is transformed in God. In this transformation the soul drinks of God in its very substance and its spiritual powers."

No words can convey the exact experience of which St. John is writing—for words are only symbols at best and cannot express the intangibles of cultural and personal being, much less the ineffable of spiritual experience. The bewildering and baffling images of Spain, and of England, such as divine darkness, cloud of unknowing, night of the spirit, could not and did not find expression in France. The French use these extravagant

[122]

terms such as annihilation, prostration, total abandonment, purely in a metaphorical sense. The lucid French intelligence either rejected the Spanish terms or transformed them. Nevertheless, the influence of St. John of the Cross found expression coming through St. François de Sales and François de Fénelon and hence into the mystical theology of France.

If St. John of the Cross influenced the thinking of the French mystics, it was the influence of St. Teresa, whose writings were translated into French early in the century, that reformed the conventual life of France and added weight to its social ethic. She never lost her sense of the social character of Christ. Such awareness of a relationship with humanity has often saved inner religion and psychological introspection from the dangers of passivity.

One of the most strenuous achievements of Cardinal Bérulle was to bring into France the first company of Carmelite nuns, an undertaking which took him several years since he refused to accept any but the best—as nearly like St. Teresa herself as he could find. Mère Anne, who was contemporary with the foundress and records the beginnings of the Order in France, described the cardinal as one with "saintly acumen and gentle obstinacy." When he had at last assembled the little company it required five Frenchmen and two Spanish monks to accompany the perilous journey "on horseback, in carriage, by boat and walking often." Mère Anne continues: "Think what poor women must suffer on so long a journey to expose themselves to people's gaze or to accept any chance help in extricating themselves from dizzy heights or deep mire. . . . If you could see what I bear from the servants of Señor Don Juan. When I tell him of my trials he replies, 'Speak not thus, my mother, we shall all die here!' and he does nothing at all but porter's work. . . . It is a bath of rose water to him when we have to suffer," and as she writes the intrepid woman has "to shake an icicle off her pen."

Mère Anne found her French daughters imbued with the teachings of Dionysius and "refined, less hard on themselves than their Spanish sisters" and also unused to the spontaneous joy of St. Teresa's daughters. Bremond remarks that the Carmelite nuns did not bring their foundress's tambourine but they brought her sense of humor. They set themselves to work to found new Orders and reform old ones. They stripped away the satin bed-gear and ornate tapestries that royalty had showered on these holy hostels, and through it all there flowed a vigorous good humor and sometimes even ecstasy. When Dijon was founded—that convent which offered Jeanne de Chantal her first spiritual home and was the pride of Bossuet's early days—"Mère Anne led her daughters to the Blessed Sacrament, with such transports as those of David before the Ark; this venerable Mother, more like a seraph than a mortal creature, passed in rhythmic dance along the choir, singing and clapping her hands after the Spanish manner, but with such a majestic sweetness and gravity that all were led into transports of joy."

Through Dijon there is almost a touching of hands between St. Teresa and those mystics who centered around the court in

Versailles. Jeanne de Chantel had been initiated into the spiritual life by François de Sales and together they mingled the
searching mystical longings of St. John of the Cross with the
system of St. Ignatius of Loyola.

St. François de Sales softened Spanish asceticism even while
he upheld St. John's high abandonment of the soul to God; he
modified the Ignatian method of prayer, giving scope to the free
soul, even while he safeguarded it from the chartless paths of
the Quietists, whose writings were beginning to circulate in
Paris. Dom John Chapman remarks, "St. John of the Cross is
austere but St. François de Sales teaches exactly the same thing
in a more cheerful manner." He, like Fénelon, saw both sides.
Fénelon was thoroughly imbued with the Salesian method of
spiritual direction and throughout his life recommended the
maxims of de Sales as themes for meditation and incentives for
self-conquest. Both had a common vocation as spiritual directors to the nobility and persons of the world. Both set forth
the life of meditative prayer for all persons, saying that, while
everyone does not have the gift of introversion, "even the dull-
witted can strive to attain it as much as he deserves." Either
Fénelon or de Sales could have written this sentence, "Those
who live in towns, in households, at the very court, who by
reason of their circumstances are obliged to live an ordinary life
in outward show . . . can live in the world without receiving
any worldly taint, can find springs of sweet piety in the midst
of briny waters of the world and can fly among the flames of
earthly passions without burning the wings of the holy desires
of the devout life."

De Sales' magnum opus is the *Treatise on the Love of God,*

which stands as the classic work of French mysticism. Dom John Chapman says: ". . . read it straight through, it is a system, the greatest work of genius in theology since St. Thomas and one of the most learned."

It gathers up mystical theology and presents it in French thinking. Dionysius describes the soul's movement as being "from goodness, through goodness, to goodness." St. François describes the saint's movement as a double action—which he calls affective and effective love. By affective love the soul breathes in the gentleness of God and by effective love it breathes out that gentleness to creation, an experience he exemplifies in his own life.

François de Sales died in 1622. On his feast day, January 29, 1700, François de Fénelon wrote to the Comtesse de Montbéron, "The feast of St. François de Sales is a great feast . . . He counted the world as nothing. You will see by his *Letters* and his *Life* that he received in the same peace, and in the same spirit of annihilation, the greatest honors and the hardest contradictions. His artless style displays an amiable simplicity, which is above all the graces of a worldly spirit. You see there a man who, with the greatest penetration and a perfect nicety in judging of things as they are in themselves, and knowing the human heart, thinks only of speaking as a good kind man, to console and enlighten his neighbor and help in the work of perfection. No one knew better than he did what the highest perfection was; but he made himself little with the little ones, and never despised anything. He made himself all things to all men, not to please every one, but to gain every one, and to gain them all for Jesus Christ and not for himself. This is the spirit of the Saint, madame, which I wish to see poured out upon you."

In seventeenth-century France two factors opposed the further development of mystical theology. On the one hand, a cynical intellectualism and avid rationalization of all mysteries was in process, and the keenest intellects of France were turning away from religion. On the other hand, the rigid observance of formalities in the Church and a superstitious devotion to objects of worship inclined the spiritually hungry to place an unbalanced emphasis on the quietistic phase of mystical experience. Quietism arose in France out of the same need as among the Quakers in England: a necessity for firsthand experience of spiritual sources.

Baron von Hügel discusses at length the development of Quietism in his great work, *The Mystical Element in Religion.* There are, he says, in the human soul four basic hungers that can be satisfied by the quietistic phase of the mystical experience. First, relatedness and unity are essential to man and whenever the earthly order becomes a collection of unmeaningful things and the multiplicity of ritual and form extreme, the spiritually sensitive become exceedingly unhappy and hunger insatiably for the One that embodies All. As the culture becomes more and more analytical and diverse the more insistent is this drive within the souls of the intensely religious until they, not without danger, leave off all outward form. Equally important to the human soul is its rooted sense of immortality—the sense that within it is something alive that will not tolerate death. Whenever society becomes predominantly materialistic and worldly, this inborn spirit asserts itself as a deep-seated passion to purify one's self from worldly affairs—to withdraw, to become detached, to practice austerities.

The third of these natural inclinations of the soul, and deeper than either of the other two, is man's capacity for awe, trust, and faith. It is essential for man to believe in something that is totally Other—an Absolute beyond finite comprehension, One whose Presence is overwhelming. Man has to worship, for only as he does so can he find the renovating power of the universe. When cynicism and skepticism are rampant the instinct of awe makes itself felt among the spiritually minded.

Paralleling this sense of awe in man is found a sense of shame at his own inadequacy in comparison with the adequate being God intended him to be. He is overcome with humility when he realizes that he has been appropriating the universe, so to speak, for his own selfish ends—the *I* assuming the proportion of God himself. The growing sense of shame results in a deep effort at self-abnegation; and as the sense of power and goodness of the Eternal increases he forgets his own activity to achieve the Presence of God and he is convinced that "my seeking him was only his seeking me." Hence it happens that when individualism, self-sufficiency, and aggressiveness characterize an age, the mystic swings far over into passivity and lays more emphasis on the receptivity of his soul and the inactivity of his own will.

It was in the very nature of things that quietism should arise in both England and France, since in both countries the official religion was a block rather than an avenue to the fulfillment of these basic spiritual hungers. In England, however, a large portion of the movement was preserved and developed into the Religious Society of Friends because of the nature of its leaders. Early in its history George Fox recognized that an ethic embodied in a group discipline was required if the spiritual movement was not to degenerate into a temporary and ineffectual anarchy, such as had occurred in the case of the Ranters, a contemporary group. With this balance to offset the dangers of quietism the Quakers were able to appropriate the quietistic principles rejected by Catholicism and use them creatively in the world. Howard Brinton, modern authority on Quaker history and mysticism, refers to the influence of quietism on early Quakerism:

For one hundred and fifty years the passive mysticism of Molinos, Madame Guyon, and François de Fénelon dominated the Society of Friends. In those two Quietistic centuries nearly all the Quaker social pioneering was done in such fields as religious freedom, equality of the sexes, equal respect for all races and classes, the abolition of slavery, prison reform, the use of non-violence in mental hospitals, peace and education. Quietism appears to be an aid not a hindrance to social pioneering, a paradox when we consider that Quietism is an effort at detachment from the world.

The reason for this positive result of an apparently negative attitude becomes evident when we consider that the pioneer, whether in religion, science, social betterment or any other field, must detach himself from the conventional if he is to discover the unconventional; he must detach himself from his self-centeredness, his own possessions (including his theories), if he is to find that Truth which is not just his own but is

universal. Whether or not the Quietist has set himself an impossible
task in seeking a Wisdom of this World he at least puts himself in that
attitude which is essential to all progress from the accepted to the
unaccepted. Without some degree of detachment from the old, discovery
of the new is impossible.

The followers of Miguel de Molinos in France were not
great mystics as were St. Teresa and St. François de Sales or
they would have realized that pressed to their conclusion these
quietistic elements in mysticism would be fatal to both inner
and outer relationships. Therefore, while quietism in England
reaped the rich fruit of a powerful religious body, its result in
France was the blotting out of mystical theology for nearly one
hundred years.

Much of the writing of quietists of this period, including that
of Molinos, is valid for all contemplatives, but the unfortunate
inference drawn from it is the fallacy that this emptiness in
the deep of the soul is the presence of God himself, instead
of being the means by which that living force is appropriated.
They mistake the means for the end. Molinos spoke in many
ways the language of true mysticism: "By not speaking or
desiring, and not thinking, the soul arrives at the true and
perfect mystical silence wherein God speaks with the soul,
communicates himself to it, and in the abyss of its own depths
teaches it the most perfect and exalted wisdom."

Miguel Molinos, a Spanish nobleman, was the same age as
Bossuet. In 1675, while Bossuet was preceptor to the dauphin,
and counseling the Duchess de la Vallière to enter a Carmelite

convent, the famous *Il Spirituelle Guida* was published. Its doctrine was approved by four Inquisitors and in six years it had gone through twenty editions and was translated into every language in Western Europe. Its author became a sort of St. Paul to devotees who considered him divinely sent not only to liberate the people from idol worship and burdensome ceremonies, but also to guide them straight into the tranquility of God himself. Innocent XI gave him lodgings at the Vatican and from there he penetrated into the whole Western religious world. In fifteen years he accumulated some twenty thousand letters and, as one contemporary writer expresses it, "everyone, the devout and those who wished they were devout, took up his simple way to holiness." Cardinal d'Estrées, Louis XIV's representative at Rome, put him in touch with important people in France, and was instrumental in having the little guidebook translated into French. Cardinal Petrucci, the Molinos exponent in France, had spiritual treatises based on *The Spiritual Guide* written for nuns. Bishop Gilbert Burnet wrote from Italy in 1685: "The new method of Molinos doth so much prevail in Naples that it is believed that he hath over twenty thousand followers in the city. . . . The best method of prayer is to retire the mind from gross images and so to form an act of faith and thereby present ourselves before God, and then sink into silence and cessation of new acts and let God act upon us, and so to follow his conduct. . . . Molinos thinks this is not only to be proposed to such as live in religious houses but even to secular persons, and by this he hath proposed a great reformation of men's minds and manners . . . The Jesuits have set themselves against this conduct as foreseeing it may weaken the empire that superstition hath over the minds of people . . . that this might breed a schism in the Church . . . It is certain that the Pope understands the matter a little and that he is possessed of a great opinion of Molinos' sanctity."

Twelve years after its publication the Roman See became alarmed and issued a circular letter to all prelates instructing them to break up all associations of quietists. That same year Cardinal d'Estrées was forced to reverse his opinion through pressure from Versailles and to press for the condemnation of *Il Spirituelle Guida.* Molinos was arrested and for two years waited in prison while the Inquisitors pried into all twenty thousand of those letters and pored over innumerable private papers. In November of 1687 they had piled up sixty-eight propositions by which they could condemn the quietist leader. "These propositions in the opinions of our aforesaid brothers, the cardinals of the holy Roman See and Inquisitors General, are judged heretical. We have therefore condemned, noted, effaced as heretical, suspicious, erroneous, scandalous, blasphemous, offensive to pious ears all writings of Miguel de Molinos. We have forbidden each and every one to speak of them, to believe, teach, keep, and practice them." A solemn warning against any further experimenters with mystical prayer! Molinos was condemned to the Vatican dungeon, where he remained the rest of his life. Within two weeks more than two hundred men and women in Rome who were suspected of quietistic prayer were arrested and examined, and some were imprisoned.

The ruthless suppression and cruel injustice of the antiquietistic movement of the period indicates the extent to which the popular scare and panic had gone. Certain alarming factors were appearing which justified in a measure the church's effort to guide this spiritual force. Spiritual directors and confessors were discovering that an excessive use of the prayer of quiet led to a barren waste and unfruitful self-concern among their penitents. They found that spiritual energy was being dissipated by scruples and fears of distraction.

The tendency to give up vocal prayer and the traditional practices of the church in many cases meant throwing away the individual's only safeguard against self-delusion. The prayer of peaceful expectation, of brooding love, was right and useful, the great saints and contemplatives of the church had said all down the ages, but only when it left the one practicing it strengthened to act and suffer and devote himself more and more selflessly to the needs of humanity. Nonmethodical prayer was unsafe for those who were not advanced in the spiritual life.

In some groups of quietists a scorn of morality had brought about great mischief. The dignity of the person was denied and the conscious life was given up to ecstatic visions and fanatical promptings so that any sense of right and wrong, high and low, was blurred. The only basis of right and of truth, they held, was in the immediate revelation, and every impulse to act that surges up from within was a revelation of divine Will. The moral system of Sinai and the ethic of the Sermon on the Mount were no more revelations of the divine Mind than the present promptings of one's own heart.

All these dangers are implicit in mystical prayer, yet, on the other hand, through its practice great souls have developed—men and women who have been given both wisdom and power to come back from their vision of God and take up the refractory elements in the world and weave them into the divine design. Their achievements of soul have not come along easy paths, there was for them no empty "will-lessness," no whimsical freedom, but rather a single intent of will and a freedom founded on eternal truth, which enabled them to be instruments of God in his creation.

"I know full well," Fénelon wrote to the regent of France, the Duc l'Orléans, "that men misuse the doctrine of pure love and resignation; I know that there are hypocrites who, under cover of such noble terms, overthrow the gospel. Yet it is the worst of all procedures to attempt the destruction of perfect things from a fear that men will make a wrong use of them."

As a Lighted Lamp

I THINK nothing either true or false, I do not even doubt, because I do not judge at all, but I go outside, pass by them respecting what I do not know. Thus, it is not for these things that I hold to you, value you, I hold to you by way of Pure Faith. All the rest is beyond me and concerns states of soul from which I am far removed. While I do not judge, it is none the less certain that I do not abstain from it without any effort or even by a certain natural prudence. No, I simply feel all these things are very easy for God and in consequence very believable.... I fear that you go too fast, that you take all the sallies of your vivacity for divine impulses and that you omit the most obvious precautions in temporal affairs, it is hard for me to think that you do not make occasional *faux pas*. However, these are small things, affecting little the real worth of our bond."

In this vein François de Fénelon responded to Jeanne Marie de la Motte-Guyon when she challenged his faith in her supernatural experiences. Such a generous and equitable viewpoint is uncommon among her biographers. She has been condemned and sainted and made ridiculous for more than two hundred years. She is portrayed as hysterical or holy, or both, depending on the temperament of her judges from the time of Bossuet and Fénelon onward. She herself would say, "The language of love is barbarous to him who loves not, but very natural to him who loves" or "I know that I have faults but I cannot be sorry for them, they are useful to make known what I am myself."

In July, 1688, on his return from the Saintonge mission, Fénelon made a detour to visit the village of Montargis, the home of Mme. Guyon. Two months before his visit Miguel de Molinos had been committed to the Vatican dungeons, and since Paris shared in Rome's excitement, Fénelon may have been on a mission of inquiry into the nature of her teachings. He had heard from M. d'Arenthon, bishop of Geneva, concerning the affairs of Mme. Guyon and Père La Combe in his diocese, and was acquainted with *Short and Easy Method of Prayer*, her first published work. Churchmen generally held it in suspicion. Critical Fénelon may have been, but he was also weary after the Saintonge mission and the inner conflict it had entailed. He knew he was not all he ought to be nor all God commanded him to be. Mingled with his aloofness from pseudo mysticism was a docile seeking for truth. Whatever he found at Montargis was sufficient to soften his attitude toward the woman he was so soon to meet on his return to Paris, where she was then living with her three children.

Montargis stands on a moist and wooded stretch of country northeast of Orléans and south of Fontainebleau, near Paris. Here forty years earlier Jeanne Marie de la Motte had been born of wealthy and devout Catholic parents and it was in its environs that she had spent the first twenty-eight years of her life. An eight months' child and sickly, she was given over to a wet-nurse by her mother who lavished her maternal affection on her handsome son, later the greedy and overbearing Père de la Motte. Like neglected children the world over, Jeanne fashioned a fantasy world. She called hers heaven and hell. By strange and fantastic martyrdom she attempted to give her dreams reality and at the same time attract to herself the affection and attention that she felt her right. To a degree she succeeded. When very young she read François de Sales and Jeanne Françoise de Chantal and learned how to make *oraison*, an unassailable refuge and one by which she became noticed and acceptable to religious people, who thought of her she says as a spiritual prodigy. When seven years old she was sent to a convent to be with an older sister. Upon her return five years later her family were pleased with her beauty and intelligence and took immediate steps to introduce her to society, with the intention of making a wealthy marriage for her.

When she was fourteen she was married to M. Guyon, two days after her eager and somewhat domineering parents had introduced her to him. He was an exceedingly wealthy merchant, twenty years her senior, who had bad health, a domineering mother, and a possessive servant. The Guyon family was conservative and commonplace in their household arrangements and had no sympathy or understanding of the refinements of personal religion—a grim setting for an imaginative intelligent adolescent with all the psychological problems of an insecure childhood. If Jeanne de la Motte had delighted in the punishment she inflicted on herself as a child, she reveled in the inner and outer martyrdom of her married life. Bad health, a bedridden and peevish husband, a heartless mother-in-law, an insolent servant, and many pregnancies, stirred in her young soul a repugnance as well as hatred and violence that were unacceptable and inexpressible in the holy life to which she had already set herself. Buried guilt tormented her day and night and drove her to revolting and painful penances. Unlike William James's healthy-minded souls, the confessional and its absolution did not give her clean, fresh feelings.

She longed to be loved and to be lovely, but she was neither. She could not trust human love and was not able to accept divine love. "I was alone and helpless in my grief," was her constant complaint. She was born close "to the pain threshold and the slightest irritant" sent her over into "sore weeping." She was by no means a delightful companion in an invalid household and failed continually in meeting the expectations of her husband. Ever more lonely, she turned to books, especially to Thomas à Kempis's *Imitation of Christ.* Afterward her life became a series of self-conscious renunciations and reflections on her manifold sins, which she scrupulously listed. More and more she turned inward and lost touch with her outward re-

sponsibilities. One day her husband sent her to observe and
report on the state of the garden; she went ten times before
she could give him a proper account. When she was seventeen
she met a Franciscan monk returning from a five-year retreat.
He spoke straight to her unhappy condition when he said,
"Seek God in your heart." It was a phrase she had read and
heard hundreds of times but the meaning came to her sharply
and suddenly as though supernaturally. "I had sought God as
though by mercenary purchase of external service . . . I felt
at this instant deeply wounded with the love of God." The
words are set down with convincing sincerity. Whatever it was
that the Franciscan monk had found in five years of solitude, of
self-discipline, of aspiration to the love of God, it communicated
comfort to her sore spirit for a time.

Her religious exercises became more and more incessant, her
ecstasies more and more profound, and her outward behavior
more and more irritating to the Guyon family. The drive of her
lonely soul to belong, to find a relationship with the highest,
was almost unbearable for all concerned. Never having received
love, she was unable to appropriate the abounding goodness of
the divine. In spite of all she said about loving God and his
loving her, her words resembled those of the little girl's fantasy.

There is an unself-consciousness about the saints that gives
them the appearance of being at home in the vicissitudes of
life. They are able naturally to abandon themselves as does the
swimmer who moves confidently along in the water. This was
the security of being for which Jeanne de la Motte-Guyon aspired but which she did not possess in spite of all her words to

the contrary. Her fears and insecurity, however, compelled her to claim the mightiest aid and most magnificent indulgence of an abundant Providence that her imagination could conjure. She claimed the whole universe as her personal support and servant; the sun and rain, friend and foe, all were God's unique dispensation for her peculiar need and convenience. She read herself into every event of history and the universe. God punished those who were unkind to her and rewarded those who obeyed her.

Spontaneity was lacking in her at this stage. Her husband's irritability was countered with a self-righteous silence; menial services were performed in a spirit of self-complacent martyrdom; family censure was answered with elaborate self-justification or floods of self-pity; the hateful animosity of her mother-in-law was endured with a conscious piety. She knew no tranquillity of spirit.

When she was twenty-two another high point occurred in her spiritual journey. As she was walking toward Notre-Dame a shabby pedestrian stopped her and urged upon her a life of pure holiness since "God required her especially for Himself alone." From that hour she resolved to be wholly His and to render absolute obedience to any leading that might suggest itself to her spirit. But such resolution, regardless of how vehemently she declared it, was insufficient to rid her of egotism. As her marriage became continually more obnoxious to her she was impelled to release herself from its onus; since this was not possible outwardly, she succeeded in escaping by seeking to make an inner union with Christ. She drew up a marriage contract, pledging her loyalty to the Lord. "Pledged as I am to be His I accept as a part of my marriage-portion the temptations and sorrows, the crosses and the contempt which fell on Him." From then on her reveling in martyrdom increased. "Since that time crosses have not been spared me, and although I have had many previously I may say they were only a shadow of those I have had to suffer in the sequel."

After another six long years M. Guyon died and his suffering wife was freed to attend wholly to her spiritual affairs. She was left with a large fortune and three children, all of which she very capably managed. But now that she was free a greater misfortune than ever befell her. An inner sadness and weariness possessed her. Her spirit, self-sustained in spite of her profession of being divinely aided, was slack and lifeless as a violin string stretched too tightly for too long. Lassitude and stupidity alternated with fear and desolation. Long-buried guilt haunted her and undreamed-of temptations confronted her. While in the depths of this spiritual mire she attended mass in the near-by monastery at which Père La Combe, a Barnabite priest, was officiating. During that single mass the darkness was dispelled and a new day dawned. The stupor of her soul was swept away.

Conversion experiences are mysterious, not only to psychologists and theologians, who apply analytical methods to them, but also to the one converted. Voices and light, power and ecstasy, are real and not imaginary experiences. William James says: "There are only two ways in which it is possible to get rid of anger, worry, fear, despair and other undesirable affections. One is that an opposite affection should break over us, and the other is by getting so exhausted with the struggle that we have to stop—so we drop down, give up, don't care any longer. Our emotional brain centres strike work and we lapse into a temporary apathy . . . this state of temporary exhaustion not infrequently forms part of the conversion experience. So long as the egoistic worry of the sick soul guards the door, the expansive confidence of the soul of faith gains no presence. But let the former faint away and the latter can profit by the opportunity, and, having once acquired possession, *may* retain it. Carlyle's *Teufelsdröckh* passes from the everlasting *No* to the everlasting *Yes* through a center of Indifference . . .

"It is natural that those who personally have traversed such an experience should carry away a feeling of its being a miracle rather than a process. Voices are often heard, lights seen, and visions witnessed. . . . It always seems after the surrender of the personal will, as if an extraneous power had flooded in and taken possession."

Without rescuing affection and redeeming human love there seems no better way for the miserable neurotic soul to right itself and come through to peace than by setting itself to love God, and no matter how inconsistent its outward behavior in relation to this ideal, if it continues persistently to grope in the dark inevitably comes the reward of light.

From this time onward Mme. Guyon used the term "I was compelled . . ." a liberation, a victory, a conviction of supernatural presence invigorated her. Montargis was to be left behind and a great evangel begun. With her renewal of spirit came a renewal of physical beauty and the magnetism of a kindled spirit. Arranging for two of her children and taking the youngest with her, she began an eight-year pilgrimage. She offered no explanation for her journeys other than the drawings of the Spirit and the circumstances of fate. Her footsteps, however, followed a trail already made by Père La Combe. She was in Geneva for five years, sometimes in the convent and sometimes in her own lodgings. She was continually busy, speaking, writing, counseling and inspiring nuns and others with her new orisons and often a particular trial to the resident clergy.

While in Grenoble *Moyen court de faire oraison* flowed freely from the pen that she believed to be guided. This is the best of all her works. In it are outlined the degrees of prayer and the method of attaining "silence of soul." "Every Christian can elevate himself by meditation . . . to silence in the presence of God, in which the soul without being inactive acts no longer except by divine impulse. Orison then becomes a perpetual, unique, uninterrupted act, by which the soul is plunged continuously into the Ocean of Divinity. The simplest are the best fitted for it. Instead of overburdening souls with so many external practices and meaningless objects and prayers, let curés instruct the poor peasants to seek God in their hearts . . . The shepherds guarding their flocks would have the spirit of ancient anchorites, and the laborers following the plow would converse happily with God and all vice would soon be banished and the kingdom of God realized on earth . . . for a few elect there is a higher perfection, a more complete passivity in which the

Divine fire consumes all impurity within us. One may arrive at the possession, not of the gifts of God, but of God Himself in this life and thus pass into a state of deification . . . to a new and wholly divine life."

The deeply religious were fascinated by her method; sincere seekers and others merely intrigued by mystical experiences heard her gladly—all this in spite of bishops and Jesuit confessors. The bishop of Geneva, alarmed by the enthusiasm of the nuns, chagrined that an uneducated woman should direct souls, and warned by outbreaks of illuminism in various provinces, ejected her from his diocese. At Grenoble, Marseilles, Genoa, Vercelli, wherever she went, the story was the same. From early morning until late at night she held open house. She believed herself to be truly an apostle sent to teach a world weary of inadequate methods, new ways of prayer. By prayer she meant—the application of the soul to God. "I told them routes by which I had passed. God knows what joy I had at it." Her natural charm, her vivid eloquence and her new-found freedom, made her the idol of young nuns. She had countless disciples during her lifetime and many more in the years that followed.

In 1686, while the Molinos trials were in progress, Père La Combe came to Paris and Jeanne de la Motte-Guyon soon followed. The archbishop de Harlai was already alert to the dangers of their teachings, for bishops had written him accusing these two of theological errors and even of immorality. Louis XIV, with his growing unease of conscience and superficial turning toward religion, was busy pressing for the condemnation of Molinos, therefore it is unlikely that de Harlai would lose any time in stamping out any semblance of quietism in his own diocese. All the clergy of France were alert and suspicious, accounts of mystical extravagances in the provinces were being received in Paris. The average Catholic householder attended his Mass and read his prayer book and was undisturbed by such unworldly matters. But for those spiritually minded Catholics in small cells and in monasteries and convents the situation was alarming. One of the most disquieting incidents occurred at Dijon, the home of Jeanne de Chantal. Mme. Guyon had visited there for a day or two before her return to Paris. She left some of her pamphlets, but already the Burgundian quietists had published their own *Maximes*. The entire congregation was so thoroughly imbued with absorption of the self in God that they had eliminated the church's sacrament of penance altogether. One sees the peril to conventional thought.

Although no complicity between La Combe and Molinos was ever established, he was under the Molinos cloud and in the same year was arrested and imprisoned at Lourdes high in the Pyrenees, where he lived for twenty-seven years. A few years after his incarceration he became insane. Jeanne de la Motte-Guyon, who had traveled ten years in the shadow of Père La Combe, quite naturally fell under the Molinos cloud as well, and although there is not the slightest evidence that she was ever associated with the famous quietist, she too was restrained by Archbishop de Harlai in the Convent de la Rue Antoine.

Her devotion to spiritual affairs was unquenched and she eventually won over the entire convent. The superior, con-

vinced of her integrity and goodness, carried her case to Mme.
de Maintenon. That lady had already been approached by Mme.
de Maisonfort, her protégée at Saint-Cyr, and the Duchesse de
Béthune, who had been an early spiritual adviser of Mme.
Guyon in Montargis days. The prophetess of *pur amour* was
released and made much of among these ladies at court.

Mme. Guyon, who lived in her inner house and ignored the
outer, and Mme. de Maintenon, who lived in the splendor of
her outer palace and could not ignore her inner mansion, were
both too emotional, too feminine and too discontented in
either of their residences not to make trouble. One was married
in spirit to the Lord himself, she thought, and the other to the
king of France, but both natures demanded a spiritual companion of the opposite sex. Both were lonely women and Fénelon had a gift for sympathy. But he also had had a Saint-
Sulpician training and clung to ideals of objective relationships
and devotion to the church, and to put aside personal desires
was a long-established habit with him.

There was a likeness and an unlikeness between the two
women. Each discovered in the other the unlived part of her
own nature and consequently each admired and mistrusted the
other. Mme. de Maintenon was demure, cold, and discreet;
Mme. Guyon was vivid, warm, and indiscreet. One was a conservative and cautious, the other was liberal and rash; one was
set to convert the king and the other had an unrestrained passion to teach the kingdom itself to pray; one could calculate
the next moves, the other dashed headlong into the hands of

her enemy; one was successful and unhappy in the palace and the other was to be unsuccessful and serene in the Bastille.

Early in her friendship with Fénelon in the Nouvelles Catholiques days Mme. de Maintenon had written of her new-found abbé: "Your Abbé de Fénelon is very well received but the world does not do him justice. He is feared and he wishes to be loved and is lovable." As she came to know him better, however, she found in his religion hope and companionship and as they met week after week at the Hôtel de Beauvilliers his spiritual mentorship gave her confidence in prayer even while it increased her unhappiness with the inane formalities of Versailles. She discovered that Fénelon's devotion to spiritual affairs gained for him an increasing popularity whereas her own inner ardor gave her increasing dissatisfaction. She gives a dreary account of herself: "A frightful blank remains in all conditions, anxiety, listlessness, craving for something else, because nothing is entirely satisfying . . . The regret of never hearing reasonable conversation is almost to kill me. For eight days I have had no relief. The pea chapter still lasts; the longing to eat them, the pleasure of having eaten them, the delight of eating them again, are the three points that have engaged us for three days. There are ladies who, having supped with the king, and supped well, have peas to eat at home in defiance of indigestion: it is a fashion, a rage—and one thing follows another. You have some strange lambs."

For Mme. de Maintenon there could be no abandonment. The "Queen of Prudence" must of necessity learn to say "No" to the natural longings of life. Such denial was a long habit with her. It had won out in the hard battles with M. Scarron and with Mme. de Montespan, and was standing her in good stead now in her struggle for power as the uncrowned queen. She had learned to listen and be silent when she wanted to speak, she had learned to influence without showing that she did so, she had learned to deny passion and friendship if they interfered with ambition. There were times when she longed to abandon herself, to take seriously the doctrine of Mme. Guyon with its passionate assent to life. She was therefore intrigued by the teaching and personality of one who seemingly accepted the daring implications of abandonment.

When Fénelon returned from Saintonge and resumed his life at court he found Mme. Guyon well established as a spiritual teacher. Their meeting was inevitable and took place at the country house of the Duchesse de Charoste at Beynes, twenty-six kilometers northwest of Versailles. Beynes was a lovely place set among the green hills near the river Mauldre. There was about it the spell of ancient holiness left by the Benedictines who long years before had contemplated and sung their Masses in a sprawling abbey not far away. In Fénelon's day the statue of St. Barbe gazed down from a wooded hill and the abbey lay in ruins. The occasion of their meeting was no small event, for it implicated all France in an ecclesiastical controversy. If Jeanne de la Motte-Guyon had remained in the convent, the quietist issue in France would have been as free of personal scandal as the Gallican-ultramontane battle. But circumstances and personalities being what they were this was impossible.

Mme. Guyon was quite overcome with "plenitude of grace"

when she first saw Fénelon. It was a momentous and happy occasion for their mutual admirers. Both were persons of remarkable distinction and intelligence. She was slight and well formed. Her portrait shows a sensitive, alert oval face with receding chin and upcurving mouth and wide upslanting eyes. Her eyes burned with an extraordinary light. Her hair is hidden by a high pleated headdress. She is wearing a dark gown with a hood that turns back into a wide draped collar, and with full sleeves edged with white ruffles of lace falling back from her beautifully tapered, slender hands. Altogether it gives a modest and graceful effect much like a half-coquettish variation of a monastic habit.

Fénelon indubitably was attracted to her, although he was not thoroughly convinced of her genuineness. On her part there were no reservations. Fénelon, with that grace of measuring his words to another's need, gave an assurance of personal recognition and respect for her that spelled companionship in an area where she was painfully lacking. Mme. Guyon had followers and admirers but not friends, and she was well aware of her lack—so much so that she could not accept anything less than a wholehearted relationship with this man who fulfilled an earlier premonition of hers.

The group of friends at Beynes that day sat in silent prayer for a time and then discussed their spiritual problems together. Fénelon and Mme. Guyon had much to say to each other. He found many points in her teachings that needed explanation. Therefore they returned to Paris together in a lumbering coach and on the long ride had ample time to discuss *pur amour*.

"As we see the clouds, thickened and driven by the south

wind, melt and turn into rain, and no longer able to contain themselves, fall and run upon the ground, mingling with and tempering the earth, so that they become but one with it; so the soul which through loving, was yet dwelling in itself issues forth in this holy and blessed stream, quitting itself forever, not only to be united with its Beloved but to be wholly mingled and made one with him."

"Love prepares its own way," said Mme. Guyon, "no other can do it for Him. He prepares our heart and leads it from fullness to fullness; he enlarges and as he enlarges, fills; for he abhors an empty heart and will run to fill it."

"This immense love pursues us in everything, and we constantly evade its pursuit. It is everywhere and we do not see it anywhere. . . . A finite love and a bounded wisdom cannot see it," says Fénelon.

"The power of pure love is an expanding one, hence the love of a beginner is not different from the saint's love, and is quite as acceptable to God. The soul gravitates by degrees into the center; the more peaceful and quiet the soul remains with no motion of its own, the more rapid is its advance. No other force is required save the weight of love."

"O love, love thyself in me," cries Fénelon. "In this way thou wilt be loved as thou art lovable. I only want to live to be consumed before thee, as a lamp burns ceaselessly before thine altars. I do not exist for myself at all. It is only thou who existest for thine own self. Nothing for me, all for thee. Better perish than allow the love which should be given to thee, ever to return to me. Love on, O love! Love in thy weak creature!

Love thy supreme beauty! O beauty, O infinite goodness, O infinite love: burn, consume, transport, annihilate my heart, make it a perfect holocaust!"

"There is a way straight to God—the short road of abandonment it precipitates into abysses, it leads we know not whither. Noble souls are led thereby with ease. There are those who when shipwrecked know how to swim, or who have perhaps seized a plank of the ship, struggle and contend for a long while before they drown; but those who cannot swim, and who have nothing to sustain them, are instantly submerged, and sinking without a struggle beneath the surface, die, and are delivered from their suffering."

When they parted Mme. Guyon said, "Do you understand now?" He answered, "It is penetrating my heart."

Jeanne de la Motte-Guyon in that irregular, almost illegible script of hers recorded the meeting in her autobiography: "Some days after my release, having heard mention of Abbé de F—— I was suddenly with extreme force and sweetness interested for him. It seemed to me our Lord united him to me very intimately, more so than anyone else . . . It appeared to me a spiritual affiliation took place between him and me. The next day I had the opportunity of seeing him. I felt interiorly that this first interview did not satisfy him: that he did not relish me. I experienced something that made me long to pour my heart into his; but I found nothing to correspond and this made me suffer much. In the night I suffered extremely about him. In the morning I saw him. We remained some time in silence, and the cloud cleared off a little; but it was not as I wished it.

I suffered for eight whole days; after which I found myself united to him without obstacle, and from that time I find the union increasing in a pure and ineffable manner. It seems to me that my soul has perfect rapport with his, and those words of David regarding Jonathan that 'his soul clave to that of David,' appeared to me suitable for this union. Our Lord has made me understand the great designs he has for this person, and how dear he is to him."

Fénelon was not insensible to her unique charm, her troubled feminity, and the sincerity of her devotion. He was deeply stirred by her words on selfless love and intrigued by her wild desire to reform the whole kingdom of France. Her persistent adherence to the spiritual path was an encouraging trait that he often missed among the ladies of the court. On the other hand, he was a skilled director of souls and knew theirs was a delicate relationship. He disapproved of some points of her doctrine as well as the indiscreet zeal with which she had followed Père La Combe. Then, too, his logical mind was offended by her loose dealings with theological truths in a dogmatic manner. The fact that he was a person of recognized intuitive powers and discernment of character is an argument against those who explain Mme. Guyon as a deluded, hysterical near-paranoiac. He was obviously influenced by her sincerity and the worth of her spiritual search. Fénelon's own integrity, his subtle insight into human relationships, his intellectual judgment, are too well established to permit of any possibility that he could find enjoyable companionship with a woman who was altogether hysterical. That something in her gropings after the light had given her value is certain.

To one as eager for genuine human relationships as was Jeanne de la Motte-Guyon, the Abbé de Fénelon's reserve implied rejection, a fact that for her was extremely painful. It is noteworthy that, while Fénelon was flexible in finding rapport with his associates, he was not effusive. "He is feared, or respected," said Mme. de Maintenon.

"Providence links us with certain people, God gives us an affection for them and we do not fear at all the desire to be loved by these people, because he who instills this desire instills it very purely, and without any return of possessiveness in us. We want to be loved as we would want someone else to be loved, if it were the order of God. We seek it for God's sake, without self-satisfaction and without self-interest . . . Before God has purified friendships, the most religious people are hypercritical, jealous, pained for their best friends, because self-love is always afraid of losing, and wants always to gain even in relations which seem the most generous and disinterested. If they do not seek wealth or honor through a friend, at least they seek a common interest, the comfort of confidence, rest for the heart, which is the greatest sweetness in life. At best they seek the exquisite pleasure of loving generously and without self-interest. . . . When it is God that we love in our friend, we stand by him firmly and with no reservations. Meanwhile if the friendship is broken in the order of God, all is serene in the depths of our souls. We have lost nothing, for we ourselves have nothing to lose, because we ourselves are already lost. If

we are saddened it is for the person we loved, in case the break
may be bad for him. The pain may be keen and bitter, because
the friendship was very sympathetic. But it is a calm suffering,
and free from the cutting grief of a possessive love."

Between Fénelon and Mme. Guyon there was a genuine comradeship differing from that which appears in the letters of any
of his other women correspondents. Here he is neither the
teacher nor the masculine helper, but at times is the learner and
at other times the companion of the way. Her moments of
mystical ecstasy are not to be doubted, experiences that were
denied to Fénelon but which he came to know more fully
through her. "I find myself in a state of peace and of communion with you that has never been greater," he wrote her on one
occasion. "Your letter gave me great pleasure, calming my ex-
cited senses and recalling me to meditation. God be thanked for
everything, and Him alone. I am devoted to you in Him with
infinite gratitude. I am extremely anxious to see you. I should
speak more circumspectly but I cannot do so with you. I did
not find Mme. de Chevreuse yesterday, but I have asked her
to arrange a day with you when she would be alone, and I will
give up all other business for this one. So don't worry about
anything. I shall have advice to ask of you. Believe me, I am
beyond all, yours in the Lord."

An exchange of letters began on the next day after the ride
from Beynes. The story of their friendship is partially told in
the one hundred and thirty-nine letters preserved from their
correspondence. M. Seitre says of Masson's edition of them:
"These letters constitute one of the most precious documents

for the study of mystic thought transmitted to us from the past. It is a three-hundred page mystical romance or dialogue of spiritual adventure, the pursuit of disinterested love by two people whose relationship qualified them to write it surprisingly well."

Her almost illegible scrawlings and his clear, even strong script indicate the character of the writers; one a mountain torrent and the other that powerful river she has described in *Torrents*. Faith and reason converse often in the letters. In her first letter, written the next day, she desired to be patient: "All my task is to obey Him blindly in all He demands of me. Oh, may He not permit that I spoil His work and daub with a miserable brush the excellent picture he would make within you, which is none other than the picture of Jesus Christ in all his beauty." Next day she had no need to wait: "It seems to me that God pours into my heart all that is necessary for you and desires his grace pass through so miserable a channel. I cannot doubt that this is all for you, for my soul is so applied to yours by God himself, that experience alone can make it comprehensible. He has decreed it so that you may be taught that his spirit is truth, and in proportion as the rest will be verified, several years hence, it will be proof to you that he wished to make use of this miserable worthlessness [néant] to communicate his mercies to you, to accomplish his design upon you. This could be frustrated only by failure to correspond. Assuredly God wishes this docility of you for a while, until he has absorbed you entirely in Himself: then it will no more be for us as the communication of a higher fountain to another, but as two rivers carried to the sea in a single bed. Assuredly it is in such a union as this that God will give you all you need."

Before he replied she had written him four letters and sent him a copy of her autobiography, a document written at the request of Père La Combe and concerning which she was in considerable doubt. Fénelon's first letter was to advise her not to burn it, "perhaps God will cause it to bear fruit in his own time and even though that fruit might be in the form of your own denial of what you have written, that would be something. In any case you wrote it in perfect simplicity and that should dissuade you from destroying it now." Here he was the director, but in the same letter he became the pupil. Having accepted the simplicity of the autobiography, he was assured that she had walked the mystic way and in that he was willing to be taught. As he explained later to Bossuet, "Mme. Guyon is only a woman but God reveals his secrets to whom he wills. If I am seeking the route from Paris to Daumartin and a peasant of the neighborhood offers to guide me I would follow him, and trust him, though he were but a peasant."

Of the one hundred and thirty-nine letters in the series all but thirty-eight are hers. In all of them there are both the naïve revelations and profound mystery of spiritual companions seeking together to lose themselves in God.

Fénelon wrote: "I never see you but in God and God through you." Mme. Guyon wrote: "There is no one on earth for whom I feel more intimate, a more continuous union, so that it seems to me sometimes that God wishes to make a single soul of yours and mine," and then she asked, "Do you feel something like this?" Fénelon wrote: "I think of you often and I

feel myself at one with you in Him who is all," and again,
"There is no distance in God, all that is one in Him touches."

Mme. Guyon replied in her usual extravagant style: "It is
His will that I tell you there is a bond between us as intimate
as it is inexplicable so that it seems that I often yes, continuously engender you in Christ." "I cannot be to you what you
are to me, but such as I am it is united to you without reserve
and as to nought else in the world," responded Fénelon.

"To those who explain all restlessness within the human
heart in terms of nerves, glands, repressions, and the subcon-
scious," wrote Gilbert and Pope in *The Abbé and the Lady*,
"the nature of the bond which drew and united these two spirits
to each other will offer no mystery and the metaphors with
which they clothe their meaning will seem transparent veils
drawn over the flesh . . . Like Adam after the Fall they will
have nothing to say but, Lo! I am naked . . . Yet the breathless
silence of time, the enfolded mystery of the human heart, its
mystic instancy, the graylight of dawn above the beckoning
frontiers where Flesh and Spirit are but shadow and substance
of the Eternal One—for all this there is no easy explanation.
The torrents of which the lady wrote empty at last into the
sea, but they flow through human hearts. It is a far journey but
let us remember, says the Pilgrim's Script, that nature though
heathenish reaches at her best to the footstool of the Highest."

The abbé wrote: "I have little spasms of doubt about you,
but they are transient." The lady replied: "Why not? I often
have them myself."

Not only were there these letters full of their pursuit of disinterested love, their longings and aspirations, but there were others in which they sought to convince each other of another point of view. In Fénelon's letters there is manifest an effort to find beneath her vagaries and extravagances a deep truth that he felt to be there. He was not always convinced that her reckless abandonment to pure instinct was the correct method and could not trust himself to its leadings. She wrote him long discursive missives on abandonment such as this one:

"So far as choice and deliberation are concerned in the case of a person already in grace, that is a person who is dead to all sense of ownership of his own soul, it is always God who appears and the first thought, or rather, simple *penchant* or instinct of a thing is from Him . . . There is need of extreme flexibility in His hands, in order to lose all direction by reason." He replied: "I feel irresolute between these two [abandonment to instinct and direction by reason]. I see reasons on both sides and have no distinct choice in the matter. Must one take the stand that embarrasses nature? The experience of certain first movements I have followed and in which I have afterwards recognized considerable of the natural, makes me afraid to act without reasoning. At other times my reasoning puts me in the greatest uncertainty."

But the one acting from a simple instinct did not argue, she simply replied: "My soul says things as a child without knowing what it says, often perceiving after it has spoken . . . I am a child abandoned to Him; I say what God prompts me to say like those mechanical heads which articulate as they are made to."

As a Lighted Lamp

The friends saw each other only rarely, mostly in the parlors of mutual friends, on the Quai des Tournelles, at the Convent of the Marmiones where Mme. Guyon was living, or at the confessional in a little chapel at Saint-Jacques-des-Haut-Pas. In planning their meetings, they took precautions against publicity. "I will be Sunday at the same time as Wednesday, you know where," wrote the lady. Owing to the circumstances of their lives, there are only two years during which they could have met. Fénelon was called to Versailles in 1689 and Mme. Guyon went that same year to live in the country with her young daughter, recently married to the brother of the Duchesse de Béthune.

It is an indication of Mme. de Maintenon's confidence in Jeanne de la Motte-Guyon that she gave her the entrée to the little spiritual group that met at the Hôtel de Beauvilliers and to that at Saint-Cyr. Mme. Guyon expanded under the warm glow of their admiration; being loved, she became more lovely. She became the oracle and had an answer for each questing soul. Mme. de Maintenon said she never wearied of listening to her as she talked of the love of God. The daughters of Colbert were fascinated and hung upon her words. Such sanction stirred her zeal and once again she revived her dreams of a spiritual army that would revitalize the church and rescue it from skeptical rationalism and formal ritualism. Her papers and manuscripts were circulated freely among these friends. *Spiritual Torrents* and *Canticle de Canticles* were added to the list.

Torrents teaches the way to the true silence of the soul. In it is a strange darkness but a grandeur of imagery and a depth of feeling that surpass her earlier volume. The *Torrents* are souls that issue from God and have no repose until they have returned and lost themselves in him never again to find themselves—they lose however neither their nature nor their reality, but their quality. "All is alike to this soul for all is like God to it. This state is not ecstasy, which causes the loss of the senses, for that attests weakness. The soul arrived at perfect life is in ecstasy without effort forever and men do not see it. The perfect soul is infallible and all creatures that would condemn it harm it less than a fly . . .

"Let your soul have within it, a continual Yes. When the heart is in union with God there is no Nay—it is Yes be it so! which reverberates through the soul. Yes is suppleness of spirit . . .

"O human sciences! ye are of so little account, and yet so much care is taken of you! O mystical and divine science! thou art so great and so necessary, and yet thou art neglected, limited, constrained and tortured! O shall there never be a school of prayer! Alas, by seeking to make a study of it, men have spoiled all. They have endeavored to give rules and measures to the Spirit of God, which is without measure."

So for two years she taught them. Sunlight shone on their little world. In August of 1689 Fénelon was appointed preceptor to the Duke of Burgundy; The Duc de Beauvilliers had been made governor a short time before and the Abbé de Langeron was installed in the royal household.

They were not unaware of the power that lay in their hands

to shape France. A revolution was planned but it was to be achieved through a new St. Louis. "All should be accomplished by an entire dependence on the movements of the beneficent Spirit," wrote Mme. Guyon in one of her last letters before Fénelon's removal to Versailles. "Be persuaded that you will see a magnificent fruit develop in its season; he will build up that which is almost destroyed and already sliding toward total destruction. . . . My heart will always be a lighted lamp which burns itself out before the Lord for the welfare of your soul, which is more dear to me than any other on earth. . . . I see already a part accomplished of what our Lord has unfolded to me; and when the rest occurs I shall say to you: Nunc Dimittis."

8

Controversy

I DO NOT know any woman to whom I would entrust myself excepting you, nor one whose opinion could detain me," replied Fénelon to Jeanne de la Motte-Guyon when she related to him her prophetic dream concerning their spiritual journey— a dream that preceded his departure from court by seven years.

She had seen herself and the abbé descending a steep mountain as the movement of the whole slope carried them with it. As they proceeded they met another woman toiling toward the summit. She approached Fénelon and detained him and the whole movement of God's will and creation itself were stopped thereby; the mountainside stood still. After a time the woman proceeded on the ascent and Fénelon then rejoined his friend. She said in her dream, "O, my child! what you made me suffer while you were with that woman!" He had answered, "I too suffered, for I was out of harmony with all about, but I am illumined by that experience, I see I am to stop for nothing in the world and shall only suffer by stopping."

This dream uncannily depicts the drama of those years at Versailles where Fénelon came to know Mme. de Maintenon more intimately and by that relationship may have delayed his own progress. He was not her spiritual director although he wrote her many letters of instruction, evidently at her own request. She confided in him the details of the life that kept her so continually occupied, her aspirations for Saint-Cyr, the boredom of the court and the difficulties of her relationship with the king. Behind the cold and calculating deeds that mark Mme. de Maintenon as a clever and an ambitious woman are these poignant and pitiful appeals to her director and her friends such as Fénelon. They reveal her hidden loneliness and deeper longings. "Consider me," she wrote, "apart from my surroundings: tied to the world, but desiring to give myself to God."

It is doubtful, however, if she allowed herself any deep affection throughout her life. Her marriage with Louis XIV was not an easy affair. He was a demanding and an exacting husband, heartless and willful. Her time, taste, devotion, and desires were constantly subject to his whim. She was not blind to his defects, and day by day they loomed larger to her as she was required to dissemble her own feelings and tolerate opinions of which she disapproved. "The king comes to my room three times a day. Everything I have to do has to be stopped to entertain him," she complained. Nevertheless, Fénelon urged patience and self-mastery upon her in regard to the king:

"The true means of drawing grace upon the king and the state is not to make a great outcry and so weary the king, but it is to edify him by dying incessantly to yourself. . . . If you speak with violence and bitterness, if you often renew the attack, if you prepare your batteries secretly . . . then you are wishing to do good in a bad way."

"I beg of God," he wrote, "that he may make your heart wide as the sea, and that he may give you through the entire renunciation of yourself a boundless expansiveness and infinite flexibility for all his designs. It is only by dint of dying to ourselves that we become ready for all things. All reference to ourselves, and all attachment to self makes the soul dry, cold, stiff and cramped. Be a child with the holy childhood of Jesus Christ; then you will be the instrument of God, who chooses weakness itself to fight against the strongest earthly power." And again: "You will see how wonderful are the hearts of those who have given themselves up, how splendid are their friendships. Their hearts are immense because they have something of the immensity of God."

Fénelon found Mme. de Maintenon's insatiable ambition to accomplish something, to be successful in whatever task she undertook, a source of distress both to herself and to her friends. He gave her constant counsel to let go, to let be, to accept things as they were. "If you will suffer the spirit of God to do with you all that is necessary . . . to cut down the deepest root of the I . . . God will enlarge your heart in such a way that you will no longer be embarrassed by the weight of any duty. Then the measure of your duties will increase with the measure of your virtues, and with the capacity of your heart; for God will give you new works to do, in proportion to the enlargement He will give your soul."

On the occasion of the feast of St. Francis of Assisi in 1689 he wrote: "I am sorry that I did not know you were called Frances, before saying Mass this morning. I wish that you may have all the humility, all the detachment, all the self-renunciation and all the pure love of God, of which your good patron has given you such an example. . . . You have need of the holy madness of St. Francis, which surpasses the wisdom of the most eminent doctors."

Nevertheless, Mme. de Maintenon made hard labor out of her progress toward God. Infinite flexibility, holy madness, and immensity of soul, were ideals buried in mystery, and to procure them she had need, said her mentor, to barter the unholy *I*, "an idol which you have not yet broken." A hard little idol this, that she never discarded. In her old age at Saint-Cyr she may have been remembering these counsels to selflessness, for she wrote: "I never wished to be loved by any particular person, I wished to be thought well of by all. I cared nothing for riches, I was far above self-seeking; all I wanted was honor. Honor was my folly, honor was my idol, for which perhaps I am now punished by excess of greatness. Would to God I had done as much for him as I have for my own reputation."

This uncrowned queen had at her finger tips two courts, one at Versailles and the other at the Convent of Saint-Cyr. The palatial buildings and richly furnished chapel stood only a few miles from Versailles and travel to and from the palace was frequent. It was a project initiated and maintained by Louis XIV—probably as a result of an uneasy conscience—and his pious wife for the shelter and education of nearly five hundred indigent daughters of the nobility. Saint-Cyr also furnished the former governess a welcome retreat from the dismal vacuum of Versailles and gave her opportunity to exercise her passion to instruct. She kept close watch over its nuns and lay sisters, writing them many letters inpiring them to "sweetness of temper, gentleness and frankness" and urging them to be zealous in their spiritual development. She was accepted as the mentor of Saint-Cyr, a position of which she was extremely jealous. However, her busyness with the details of the institution were sometimes wearisome to herself and to those in charge. On several occasions Fénelon wrote her: "As to Saint-Cyr, I should think that an inspection, which should not descend to details, and a constant attention to regulate in this general manner all that needs regulating would be quite sufficient for a person so overwhelmed with affairs as you are. . . . A little simplicity would help you to practice virtue more usefully and with less trouble."

Early in their friendship at Versailles, Fénelon began to collaborate with Mme. de Maintenon in the work of education at the convent, often writing particular spiritual directions to the sisters there. He was not, however, the official spiritual director and confessor, an office filled by a fellow seminarian of Fénelon's, Godet des Marais, bishop of Chartres. Des Marais was also the spiritual director of Mme. de Maintenon herself.

When Mme. Guyon was released from the Convent de Marie

de la Rue Antoine, her benefactress not only introduced her to the little group at the Hôtel de Beauvilliers but also gave her the key to Saint-Cyr, a privilege that Mme. Guyon would have done well not to have accepted. The superior was her cousin, Mme. de Maisonfort, whose devotion to spiritual matters had earlier endeared her to both the Abbé de Fénelon and Mme. de Maintenon. She was an excitable and eager seeker after truth and had allowed her two friends to overpersuade her to accept holy vows. She was an ardent admirer of her cousin and had already circulated her works among the nuns at Saint-Cyr so that when Mme. Guyon actually arrived at the convent all were agog to hear her. Whenever she visited and lectured there the nuns were carried away by her counsels, and later her letters of instruction to various members were passed from one eager hand to another. Her teaching thoroughly penetrated the place; mystical phraseology became the common parlance among the sisters, states of soul, disinterested love, annihilations and trials of the holy, became their absorbing interest; The *Short and Easy Method of Prayer* interfered with other occupations of communal life—ordinary details like keeping the house or cooking the meals. Mme. Guyon became their oracle, the Abbé Fénelon their idol, and Mme. de Maintenon remained the schoolteacher.

The King's wife became alarmed by the changed atmosphere at the convent, even though she herself was in part at fault. Both her friends had advised against a free circulation of their writings, saying that an indiscriminate reading of them was dangerous and not to be permitted. She felt inadequate to deal with the wave of mystic searching that was developing among the more enlightened members of the community. However, her fears were alleviated when she discovered that Bishop des Marais of Chartres was already taking the matter in hand. He requested her to confer with Jacques Bénigne Bossuet, with de Noailles, bishop of Châlons and with the Abbé de Fénelon. All of them urged her to discretion. She wrote immediately to Mme. de Maisonfort:

"I yield heartily to the Abbé de Fénelon and M. de Chartres. I myself shall always be submissive to the opinion of these two saints. . . . My want of experience in these things set me against the Abbé Fénelon, when he did not wish to show Mme. Guyon's writings. But he was right. It is not everybody that has a sound and straightforward judgment . . . You talk perpetually of a condition of perfection and you remain full of imperfection. As for Mme. Guyon you extol her excessively. We must be satisfied with keeping her to ourselves . . . Do not be so eager, talk less, and above all things do not be carried away by your feelings. . . . These writings declare the freedom of the children of God to some who are not his children."

She then wrote Mme. Guyon requesting her not to visit Saint-Cyr, a request not too gracefully received by that lady, but faithfully obeyed. In the famous autobiography she attributed her expulsion from Saint-Cyr to jealousy of court priests. She wrote: "When these ladies and others were in the vanities of the world, when they patched and painted and some of them were in the way to ruin their families by gaining a reputation for expense of dress, nobody rose to say anything against it, they were quietly suffered to do it. When they have broken off from all this, then they cry out against me as if I had ruined them. Had I drawn them from piety to luxury, they would not make such an outcry."

About this time Mme. Guyon went to live with her daughter in the country, her writings and letters to members of Saint-Cyr were burned, and only her ideas were left there. Still an apprehension lingered in the mind of the mistress of Saint-Cyr. The court priests were exceedingly unfriendly and claimed with some reason that through Mme. Guyon's influence many of their penitents had been lured away from the confessional. No rumor of her former friend's teaching or her own implication in the spread of it at Saint-Cyr must be allowed. She therefore set about to erase every taint of the pernicious doctrine that might remain. In 1693 formal proceedings were instituted against the former seeress of Saint-Cyr. At this point, the Abbé de Fénelon was under no suspicion, but rather was more popular than ever among the courtiers.

There is no early evidence that Jacques Bénigne Bossuet had ever met Jeanne de la Motte-Guyon, for his interests had been largely preoccupied with the Gallican struggle, which he had just brought to a successful conclusion. But now he was confronted with the quietist issue through Mme. de Maintenon, who called him into the affair, and through Fénelon, who advised Mme. Guyon to take her writings to his former teacher. Bossuet was not unacquainted with the Molinos trials and the spread of quietism throughout France; in fact the spread of ecstatic mysticism had come close to him. He was a Burgundian, proud of his province and prouder of Dijon, where the two saints, François de Sales and Jeanne de Chantal had added a religious element to a province already famed for its appreciation of the good things of life. In 1689 a wave of quietism had swept through the convent there and brought into disrepute the teachings of these two canonized saints. He was not predisposed, therefore, to look favorably upon any doctrine that flavored of quietism.

Mme. Guyon, unaware of the bias of her examiner, came to him free from any distrust whatsoever. She put into his hands all her papers—letters, *Torrents, Canticle de Canticles,* and an intimate manuscript autobiography—one Fénelon himself had never seen. To her the relationship was an entirely friendly one. Bossuet took the masses of material to Meaux and settled down to give them that minute attention which was characteristic of him. It was a labor obnoxious to his nature. His mind tended to clearness; as a scholar thoroughness was essential to him and consistency was a virtue. Her inconsistencies and inconsequential detail baffled him. Here was a practical, logical, industrious man who had set himself to make sense out of the writings of an impractical, illogical, and impulsive woman.

Sainte-Beuve, in the early nineteenth century, wrote: "Of all men Bossuet has the mind that comprehends most fully, with most enlightenment, and most entirely, the world of moral, political, civil and religious doctrines, and who excels most in setting them forth with clearness, brilliancy, and splendor, looking at them with the most exalted or central point of view. Like the ruler and king of his sphere he gathers them together, develops all their springs, combines all their movements and brings forth their respective harmonies, like the stops of a huge organ in a vast cathedral nave. But at the same time, his is a mind which does not quit the nave, that well-filled sphere—a mind which feels no need to go out thence, which practically originates nothing, and never innovates. He abhors novelty, disturbance and change; in a word he is the grandest and most sovereign organ and interpreter of all that is primordial and established."

Although Bossuet continued to study throughout his long life, his reading was not an adventure into truth, but rather it was for confirmation of what he already had accepted, or it became a source of controversy with truth he held as immutable.

Mme. Guyon had another method, if so it may be called. She has described her writings thus: "I set myself to write without knowing how and I found it came to me with a strange impetuosity. What surprised me most was that it flowed from my central depth and did not pass through my head . . . I often left the meaning half-finished, without troubling myself whether what I was writing was connected or not . . . I write with incredible swiftness for the hand hardly follows the spirit which dictates and during the long work [*Torrents*] I did not change my conduct, nor make use of any book. The rapidity with which I wrote was so great that my arm became swollen and stiff. What is good in it comes from you alone, O God, and what is bad comes from me."

After six months of careful perusal of her voluminous works, the bishop of Meaux arranged to meet Mme. Guyon at the Convent of the Daughters of the Holy Sacrament. He brought

[171]

with him a well-prepared memoir listing twenty clear-cut points upon which he required a rational explanation. To him the arrangement was very plain, to her it was utterly confusing. She has described the interview: "He spoke with extreme vivacity and scarcely gave me time to explain my thoughts; it was not possible to make him change some of the articles . . . He wished me to render a reason for an infinity of things I had put in my writings, which were entirely new and unknown to me. [She often explained that she never knew what she had set on paper.] What I should have wished of the bishop of Meaux was that he would not judge me by his reason but by his heart . . . We separated very late. I left that conference with a head so exhausted I was ill from it for several days."

Jacques Bénigne Bossuet reported to the bishop of Chartres and to Mme. de Maintenon that in both content and form the works were intolerable and contained one positive heresy: the perfect should never pray for virtue for themselves because, being wholly in God's hand, their state is his concern rather than their own. "Our Lord holds me so far removed from myself or from my natural state that it is impossible for me to take a painful view of myself. When a fault is committed by me, it leaves no traces on the soul; it is something external, which is easily removed. Do not infer that I am blind to my faults. . . . Souls transformed into God have faults as a writing traced on sand when the wind is high, the wind defaces it as soon as it is traced." And again: "I love my weaknesses. They show a hidden manna under the roughest shell." How deal with such self-confidence!

In the end, although she did not follow the churchman's reasoning, she submitted to him and signed his condemnation of her works in April, 1694. She promised neither to write nor to preach, and retired once more to the country. Soon afterward she considered returning to the Benedictine convent in Montargis where she had been loved and given saintly status.

After Bossuet had examined the papers of Mme. Guyon, especially the intimate and exaggerated autobiography, full of predictions, visions, miracles, descriptive states of overwrought feeling, as well as its gropings after "pure love," he assumed the responsibility of opening the eyes of Fénelon to the dangers of friendship with its author. Bossuet's indignation was at this time directed toward Mme. Guyon, whose unwitting victim he considered Fénelon to be. He was convinced that his younger friend had failed to realize the insidiousness of Mme. Guyon's teaching and personality. Fénelon, on the other hand, had rather strangely, not anticipated their inability to find a meeting of minds and had had every confidence that Bossuet's fair judgment would discount vagaries for what they were, and would not judge where he did not know. There were psychological implications that his usually intuitive mind failed to grasp.

Bossuet pursued an absolute transcendent God; by a dynamic direction of his will he endeavored to divest himself of his evil nature—a nature other than spirit—he sought to struggle up the rigorous trail to perfection. He was the aggressor— thoroughly masculine.

Mme. Guyon felt herself to be pursued by an all-loving Providence; by giving up herself and surrendering her will, she hoped to be caught up in his love, and carried along in his strength as a little child is carried in its mother's arms. Hers was an immanent God, and she felt herself surrounded by the great ocean of his presence. God was not fixed and immutable, rather he was in the flux of things and therefore he could turn her little blunders to his own great plan. She was the recipient—thoroughly feminine.

These two opposite natures had no common symbolism. Between them stood Fénelon, skilled in the language of both. The theologian and the simple mystic were met where they stood, and just because he knew them both so well he was unaware that they did not speak the same language.

In the exchange between the two men, Fénelon held out that "spiritual directors who encounter women full of mysterious dreams, as well as ignorant men with visions, should not put them down as fanatics, nor persecute them, nor suppress them. They should neither be accepted nor rejected until their extraordinary experiences have been examined. To be ashamed of divine gifts or the folly of the cross, to ridicule facts that appear to resemble things which happened at the foundation of the Christian religion, is dangerous—since it is possible that the same Holy Spirit created them . . . the revolution of a religious revival is the need of the day, a simplicity of faith among all men, scholarly and unlearned, is France's great hope."

Mme. Guyon did not retire to the Benedictine convent in Montargis, as she had planned. She had obviously no vocation for an enclosed order and was already chafing under the restrictions that Bossuet's condemnation had imposed upon her, as well as irritated by its vague and ambiguous accusations. She requested that a commission be appointed to examine her faith and personal life. Her request was granted and she was asked to choose her examiners. She selected Bossuet, the bishop of Meaux, de Noailles, the bishop of Châlons, and M. Tronson, the venerable superior of Saint-Sulpice. Her reasons for these selections are given in her autobiography: "The first person on whom they cast their eyes was the bishop of Meaux. I was very well pleased to see him enter upon it. I had had an opportunity of explaining to him an infinity of things on which he had appeared to me satisfied . . . I did not doubt that in a quiet discussion in presence of people of consideration and knowledge, who would be equally conversant with the subject, I should at least make him change his opinion in so far as not to condemn in me what he would not dare to condemn in so many saints canonized by the church. . . . I also asked for the bishop of Châlons, de Noailles, who had mildness and piety. I thought he would have more knowledge of the things of the spiritual life and of the interior ways—and that my language would be less barbarous to him. . . . Two of my most intimate friends wished that M. Tronson should enter it."

Mme. de Maintenon had already submitted to the commission the most private counsels given to her by Fénelon, which she had written down in four little red notebooks. These were handed over to des Marais, the bishop of Chartres, her spiritual confessor, who although not formally enrolled among the members of the commission was known to be in close touch with it. It is difficult to understand this action, since at the time there were the most friendly relations between Fénelon and Bossuet. About the same time Fénelon sent a sort of "general confession" of his own faith to Bossuet.

Because of M. Tronson's age and poor health, the commission met in the country house of Saint-Sulpice in Issy, a village within walking distance of Paris. The conferences extended over a period of six months, during which time the two active prelates divided their activities between the duties of their dioceses and the great mass of material offered by Jeanne de la Motte-Guyon and François de Fénelon. At the request of the commission the latter furnished reference materials from the writings of the saints. Bossuet, who never traveled without books, would arrive with ponderous folios of mystical writings and through the long summer days the three would read aloud in the little pavilion: the logical mind of Bossuet making a thorough research, jotting down his innumerable and careful notes, gathering concrete information about an abstract and indefinable experience; M. Tronson attentively listening, finding bases for his final judgment, weighing the evidence with his impartial consideration for both sides, remaining silent for the most part; and de Noailles, the youngest of the three, speaking with unprecedented boldness at inopportune times, then finding need gracefully to trim his sails to suit the occasion.

The three worked alone except when Fénelon joined them— not officially at first but as a welcome friend. On March 6, 1695, the Articles were ready for signature but between then and the actual date of signature, four days later, they were increased from thirty to thirty-four. They were colorless and contradictory and furnished ground for a still greater controversy. Fénelon signed them reluctantly, saying he would have signed them with his blood had they been altered still further.

They restated simply the principal duties of positive Christianity and expressly forbade the exercise of any devotional practice that would destroy these duties. One article bore the stamp of Fénelon: "The prayer of simple presence of God or self-surrender and quiet, and other extraordinary prayers even passive, approved by St. François de Sales and other mystics may not be reflected upon or held in suspicion without temerity." Another article bore the stamp of Bossuet: "It is possible to become a very great saint without these extraordinary prayers . . . extraordinary ways are rare and subject to the investigation of the bishops."

For Fénelon none of his relations with the parties involved was altered and apparently he did not realize the growing animosity in the mind of Bossuet. Two weeks after signing the Articles he wrote from Versailles to his old friend: "There is nothing new here, save that you are missing and that the *philosophers* feel the change. I fancy after the festival, if fine weather comes, you will go to Germigny to enjoy the charms of spring. Tell it, I pray you, that I can never forget it and that I hope to find myself once more within its shrubberies before I go to my Belgians."

During the sessions at Issy, Louis XIV had appointed Fénelon to the diocese at Cambrai. On June 10, 1695, he was consecrated as archbishop of Cambrai in the little chapel at Saint-

Cyr by the bishop of Meaux, assisted by the bishops of Châlons and Amiens. His new responsibilities entailed his absence from Versailles for nine months of the year—a deprivation for him since not only were his friends and familiar comrades at the court, but also he could not easily sacrifice his relationship with the Duke of Burgundy to whom he was devoted and upon whom depended all the plans to spiritualize France. Fénelon's attachment to the court of Versailles is breathed forth in his later nostalgic letters from Cambrai. Mme. Guyon was aware of this attachment and felt that there was an unwholesomeness about its attraction for him. "I trust that God will remove him from a place so deadly to him, since he clings to it so . . . I hope the tempest will drive him into port and that when he shall be removed from that place he will know the repose of which his attachment is robbing him."

Mme. Guyon, who had retired to the Convent of the Visitation in Meaux, signed the Articles and also a declaration drawn up by Bossuet, stating she had never had any intention of putting forward any doctrine contrary to the church's teaching. Bossuet apparently then gave her permission to leave the convent, providing she would not return to Paris or to the court. She left so precipitately that whether erroneously or maliciously the rumor was spread that she had escaped over the convent wall. A touch of humor appears in a letter written to a friend: "In any case it would have been impossible for me to leap over a wall, since I am not a very good jumper." Whatever the truth of the matter may have been, Bossuet was more incensed than ever because of her hasty withdrawal from his guardianship to some unknown refuge. Added to this was his dissatisfaction that the Articles which he had desired to be a drastic denunciation of the dangerous doctrine of quietism had turned out to be quite spineless and lacking in vigor.

In the meantime the diocese of Paris had been left open by the death of de Harlai. Fénelon, Bossuet, and de Noailles were under consideration. Fénelon could well have been Mme. de Maintenon's selection if she had been more certain of his attitude toward Mme. Guyon. She had set herself to separate the two friends if at all possible. She wrote to de Noailles: "I saw the archbishop of Cambrai yesterday. . . . We talked about Mme. Guyon. His mind does not change concerning her; indeed, I believe he would suffer martyrdom rather than admit he is wrong." Mme. de Maintenon was worldly-wise in selecting the new archbishop—Bossuet was old and was not of a noble family; Fénelon was fluid, unpredictable as the current of a rushing river; on the other hand, de Noailles was young and more amenable to the royal will than either of the other two. Therefore it was he who became the archbishop of Paris.

A search for Mme. Guyon was begun and continued for four months, when she was discovered on Christmas Eve, 1695, in Paris and taken to the state prison in Vincennes. Fénelon had already gone to Cambrai when this affair came up again. The persistent persecution by the church might have ended at this time, for both de Noailles, then archbishop of Paris, and Madame de Maintenon herself were willing that Madame Guyon should be housed in some enclosed religious order without further oppression. Bossuet, however, would have no such disposal of the case. His confidence in his own judgment was unwavering and he was obsessed with the idea that he was defending the church against an insidious evil. Only such a passion could account for the abnormal venom with which he pursued a person whose intellectual powers and ecclesiastical standing were so far beneath his own and so unworthy of his superb abilities.

Derision by enemies and flattery from devout defenders of Mme. Guyon have so clouded the story that a fair telling of it is difficult. But all are agreed on the unhappy figure that Bossuet presented in the controversy. He descended to an emotional bickering that discredited the noble course of his earlier life. He calls forth the compassion of those who understand something of the disappointment of disillusioned old age. He was an old man who still had visions of perfection, even as he had in his youth when he made his retreats at Saint-Lazare with Vincent de Paul, or at La Trappe with Racine. Yet between the regret of the old man and the hopes of the young man there lay a span of time given over to years of self-will and self-sufficiency. Never had he been for long without the vision of perfection. In his Scriptures, his St. Augustine, his philosophers, he tasted secondhand the fruits that had been brought back from the Holy Land. Yet he had never dared to venture into those strange and dangerous lands himself. His own spiritual cowardice may account for his sensational violence in this struggle.

Whatever may have been the faults of Mme. Guyon they were certainly no worse than the duplicity of her adversaries.

If she was hypocritical—and there is more evidence against this judgment than for it—so were her accusers. Absolute purity of motive has never been allied with cruelty, for the cruel hate themselves as they hate their fellows, since in them is hidden a guilt similar to that which they decry. The would-be devout, whose fickleness is revealed by their hanging one week on her words and the next making witty sayings about her teachings and person, stand condemned by the steadfastness with which she clung to her idea of pure love. Actually the vacillating nature of many whom he directed gave justification for Fénelon's loyalty to one who was insecurely folded in the approval of the church and the court.

Her worst vices were recklessness of spirit and inconsistent theology; her independent spirit did not permit her to conform to patterned holiness. Free speech and action are dangerous errors in an absolute monarchy where hearts are already restive under an enforced uniformity of life. Above her rashness of spirit and linguistic blunders and extravagant imagery, none of which she denied, was her confidence in the love of God, a confidence that overcame her egotism, vanity, and self-interest. She was always convinced that she had a truth of which no earthly power could deprive her. In her day and ever since, through two centuries, slander has followed her, her wild writings were interpreted or misinterpreted by Freudian psychologists, and their pathological elements overemphasized. Her autobiography is full of herself, her glory in suffering, her mystical privileges, her power over places and persons, but it is also full of an infinite trust and dependence upon the divine Source.

In 1696, after a brief reprieve from the prison at Vincennes, she was committed to the Bastille. Behind twelve inches of rock wall, shut away from rain and sun, friend and foe, away from the hectic activity of writing and preaching, the torrent was brought to the stillness of a pool. When the Bastille loomed before her she wrote: "I feel no anxiety in view of what my enemies will do to me. I have no fear of anything but of being left to myself. So long as God is with me, neither imprisonment or death will have any terrors."

Five years later, when fifty-four years old, aging and ill, she was carried to the home of her daughter at Blois, a hundred miles from Paris on the Loire. Here she lived for fourteen years quietly teaching and writing. She who had been painfully sensitive to trifling slights and small bruises in her early days, in the end made little comment on the deep pain of five bleak and lonely years in a narrow cell: "I being in the Bastille said to Thee, O my God, if thou art pleased to render me a spectacle to men, thy holy will be done. . . . I am willing that all men should hate me. Their strokes will polish what may be defective in me."

The Chevalier Ramsay, a friend of Fénelon's later life, and Fanfan, the favorite nephew of the archbishop, attended her funeral. Ramsay had lived for some time in her household at Blois. Gosselin, whom Baron von Hügel considered an authority on Fénelon, said that "she is a truly saintly filial Catholic." Early in the eighteenth century the gist of her teachings, along with those of Miguel de Molinos and François de Fénelon, was published by the Quakers in a small devotional book, *A Guide to True Peace*. One hundred years before the abolition of slavery, John Woolman, with a concern to eradicate a harmful trade among Friends, followed its teachings as he went about from one slave-trading Friend to another. He did not say much about the suffering and injustice of the system; he simply set before them the fact that slaveholders could feel no inner peace. In calling their attention to this state of affairs he touched the dynamic center of all Quaker social reform.

William Blake gathered her into the company of the saints. In *Jerusalem* he has placed St. Teresa and Mme. Guyon among the gentle souls guarding the fourfold gates that open toward Beulah, the gate of the contemplative life. The two guard the great wine press of love where mankind receives the wine of life at the hands of the mystics.

Bossuet's battle with Mme. Guyon was finished, everything had gone his way. He felt that he had rescued the church from the pernicious doctrines of *Short and Easy Method of Prayer*. However, his victory did not bring him happiness; rather, it had tended to make him less sensitive to his spiritual roots. He wrote: "I tremble to the very marrow of my bones when I consider the lack of depth in myself. . . . Nevertheless, if anyone were to suggest that I was wrong in anything I should defend myself with any number of arguments. Oh, when will God be my sole desire!"

Bossuet was seventy years old, his powers were declining, and no signal ecclesiastical honor had come his way. Still, he never wavered in his zeal to maintain the status quo of the church, taking up conservative cudgels for her to the day of his death.

François de Fénelon

He saw in Fénelon a rising star and, whatever the older man's motives, whether the jealousy of an aging man or a desire to influence the policy of the church beyond his generation, for him it became essential that Fénelon publicly subscribe to his interpretation of the Articles of Issy. As they stood, the Articles did not commit the archbishop of Cambrai to the support of Bossuet. He therefore proposed to publish a treatise *Etats d'Oraison* that would embody all that he had hoped to include in the original statement. The preparation of such a book was no small task for him but with his usual industry and thoroughness he completed it by July, 1696, and sent it to Fénelon for an official endorsement. As Fénelon had suspected when he looked over the proposed statement, it was a contradiction of those portions of the Articles which he had struggled to maintain.

If the personal elements were eliminated between the antagonists, one could see enacted here the age-old conflict between mysticism and institutionalism.

Charles Bennett, in his *Philosophical Studies of Mysticism*, implies that any institution tends to think that its own existence is intrinsically valuable and thus it obscures its own purpose; while the mystic, on the other hand, cultivates a kind of originality and self-reliance that comes of being in touch with the Divine Source of Things, a temper that is dangerous to the docility required by the institution. The mystic is thus the purest type of radical and the most threatening because he feels he has God behind him. The intimate consciousness of relation to God is religion in its most acute, intense and living stage. In it is the recovery of nerve. The saint, the martyr, the mystic are feared by the adherents of the institution and are inevitably attacked by it but never conquered. George Santayana says, "It is only in contemplative moments that life is truly vital, when routine gives place to intuition, and experience is brought before the spirit in its sweep and truth." So it proved to be in the coming struggle between the bishop of Meaux and the bishop of Cambrai.

Fénelon may have been unduly sensitive in what he considered was a direct attack on Mme. Guyon's doctrines. He had continued to support her with an unchanging belief in her as a person and had stood behind her during the interrogations before and after the conferences with suggestions and methods of answering innumerable questions. When he was asked to endorse the *Etats d'Oraison* he wrote M. Tronson, requesting that he confer with de Noailles in the matter. Concerning Mme. Guyon he said: "What does it matter that I do not believe Mme. Guyon to be either mad or wicked, if I maintain absolute silence, if I leave her to die in prison without taking part directly or indirectly in anything that concerns her? They could not desire to press me further if they did not believe that some dangerous mystery lay behind my aversion to censuring her. Yet the sole mystery is that I do not desire to insult one whom I have reverenced as a saint from all I have, personally, seen of her. Can they truly have doubts of my sincerity? Have I behaved as if I calculated or dissembled? Should I be in my present difficulties if I had been influenced by the world? Why should that be required of me which would hardly be required of an impostor?"

By concurring in Bossuet's request Fénelon could have saved

himself with Mme. de Maintenon and the bishop of Meaux
for a time, but the very nature of the circumstances and the
temperaments of those involved would have made the break
inevitable as the years went on. M. Tronson and de Noailles
advised Fénelon to return the Bossuet manuscript unendorsed,
and by following the suggestion he committed an action by
which he set himself in direct opposition to his old friend and
secured the enmity of his most powerful friend at court. The
lady who was nicknamed "Votre Solidité" determined that
there should be a clean break with Mme. Guyon and all taint
of quietism erased. She did not propose to lose her friendship
with Fénelon, yet she was not prepared to face any difficulty
because of it.

In 1695 she had written "M. de Fénelon gave me the assurance that he was concerned in this affair only in order to
prevent the opinions of the truly religious from being condemned through inadvertance. He is not the advocate of
Mme. Guyon although he is her friend. He is the upholder
of Christian piety and perfection. I rely on his word for I know
few men as frank as he is." But a year later she became more
fearful and closed herself off from the little circle at the Hôtel
de Beauvilliers. In 1696 she wrote: "I have had a great deal of
intercourse with M. de Cambrai and neither of us succeeds in
persuading the other . . . The coolness between the Duchesses
de Beauvilliers and de Chévreuse and myself increases every
day." About this time Fénelon wrote her: "Why do you close
your heart to me, madame, as though I were of another religion
. . . Why fear to speak of God with me, as though you dreaded

to be misled? I go away with the hope that God who sees our hearts will reunite them, though with a deep grief at being cross with you . . ."

Again in October of that year she wrote to de Noailles, of a great argument with Fénelon, "would I were as faithful and devoted to my duty as he is to his friends."

The *Etats d'Oraison* was to be published in March, 1697. Fénelon, after consultation with M. Tronson and de Noailles and receiving their endorsement, prepared to reply with the *Maximes des Saints,* a treatise that purposed to assemble together the teachings of the saints on the doctrine of pure love, especially those of St. François de Sales. He attempted, not very subtly, to show that Mme. Guyon's tenets were not unique aberrations but were the old teachings of the saints revived. Unfortunately, through the impulsiveness of his friends, possibly de Chévreuse, it was rushed through the printers' hands and published before Bossuet's treatise. Consequently it appeared to be an undue defense of Mme. Guyon and an unnecessary publication. The public saw no relation between it and the *Etats,* which did not appear until one month later. Its publication aroused the king, who demanded of Bossuet that he procure from Fénelon a public acknowledgment of his errors. The bishop of Meaux pledged himself to secure the retraction from his former friend. A council made up of the bishop of Chartres and M. Tronson and Bossuet was called upon to confer with Fénelon. De Noailles, who had boldly endorsed the manuscript, withdrew his support and M. Tronson refused to speak in his pupil's defense until pressed to do so. He then threw in his decision with Bossuet. All three ruled that the *Maximes des Saints* was heretical and therefore every bishop in France should forbid its circulation in his diocese.

Fénelon's reaction to his former friends was varied. His admiration for M. Tronson never altered throughout his long life; for de Noailles he may have held resentment although he gave it no voice, but years later he violently opposed him in a further chapter of the Jansenist controversy. However, he held Mme. de Maintenon largely responsible for the whole affair. He wrote her at this time: "Permit me to remind you, madame, that after seeming to share our opinion on the innocence of this woman, you turned suddenly to the exact opposite. Ever since then you have been suspicious of my firmness, your heart has been closed against me; people who desire a chance of intercourse with you, and of becoming necessary to you inform you or impress upon you in roundabout ways that I am deluded, that I may be growing heretical. They resort to many methods to move you; you are struck by them, and pass from excessive confidence and security to excessive disturbance and alarm. This has been the cause of all your misfortunes. You dare not follow your own heart and your own instincts . . . If you had spoken openly to me, I could, in three days, have brought all the disturbed souls of Saint-Cyr to peace and entire submission to their saintly bishop . . . Do not fear that I shall contradict Monseigneur de Meaux; I shall never speak of him except as my master, or of his propositions but as the rule of faith. I am willing that he should triumph and that he should convict me of every kind of error; it is not a question of me, but of the doctrine . . ."

However, when friends advised him to withdraw the *Maximes* and leave the matter to settle itself he refused to do so. Now he stood almost alone, but he set himself to face the struggle with all the wisdom and self-control the years had given him. In his letters of spiritual direction during the next few years of strife there were many counsels to the higher will: "seeing in it all things, what it is and why it is."

His first move was to request permission of Louis XIV to carry his appeal to Rome, feeling that if he himself presented the doctrine it would be fairly dealt with. The king was not insensitive to Fénelon's personal power and so not only refused his plea to go to Rome but also banished him from Versailles, a decree he later enlarged to conclude his relationship with the Duke of Burgundy. Fénelon and Louis XIV had never been on easy terms, since the latter feared any independent spirit and made it a policy to remove any such disintegrating influence, either gently or otherwise. Henceforth the road to Versailles from Cambrai was forever closed. However, the little circle at the Hôtel de Beauvilliers stood loyally behind him, the Ducs de Beauvilliers and de Chévreuse never wavered in their affection and dependence upon him as a spiritual adviser. It is an evidence of the high esteem in which Louis XIV held de Beauvilliers that, although the latter made no secret of his relationship to Fénelon, the king continued to retain him as governor to the Duke of Burgundy.

The conflict moved from Versailles to Rome. In France

Bossuet's position was favorable, for on his side were Louis XIV, Mme. de Maintenon, and necessarily the entire court and the well-known churchmen. The Jesuits sided with Fénelon, even the king's confessor giving him secret approval. The reason for this partiality is evident, since Bossuet was a Gallican through and through as well as showing some Jansenist leanings. These two factors militated against the Bossuet influence in Rome, whereas Fénelon's ultramontane policy and open resistance to the Jansenists were all in his favor. Conferences began in October, 1697, and continued for nearly two years.

During the period floods of words poured from the pens of both men as well as from their personal representatives in Rome. The nephew of Bossuet fed the fires of controversy on his behalf with envenomed gossip and personal attacks, while the Abbé de Chanterac, long-time friend and relative from Périgord, carried on the battle for Fénelon in the Holy City. "In this whole affair," wrote Fénelon to de Chanterac, "the chief thing for us is to maintain patience, simplicity, and candor and to explain ourselves precisely and without reserve on each article." The Abbé de Chanterac was committed to this point of view but he was far from being astute enough to outwit the virulent elements that eventually crept into the conflict. He was too much of a gentleman to enter wholeheartedly into such a controversy.

The personal charm of Fénelon flowed through his pen. His imagination, nimble intellect, and understanding spoke more clearly to the Roman Council than did Bossuet's solid learning and cumbersome if lucid logic. As things progressed adversely for Bossuet, he became more and more convinced of a divine mission to save the church. Hysterically he wrote: "If it were not for me the whole affair would drop . . . I stand alone . . . You can do as you will but I warn you that I shall proclaim these heresies . . . I will make my voice heard in Rome and throughout the world . . . If you leave me alone none the less I will go forward, for God has shown me the peril that threatens souls and I am confident he will not desert me or his church and that truth shall prevail."

Out of such desperation Bossuet, in 1698, published the *Rélation sur le Quiétisme* which purported to be the inside story of the controversy. It was received in Parisian and Roman circles with such a commotion on both sides that the flagging interest of the public was reanimated. Mme. de Maintenon remarked, "Mme. Guyon's follies amuse the world." In it Bossuet had betrayed private conversations and implied scandals without any proved basis. Fénelon was at first reluctant to respond to the *Rélation* but after considerable counsel did so and his *Réponse* was gathered up as avidly as had been Bossuet's provoking treatise. Bitterness was not lacking on either side, although Fénelon was more subtle than his opponent and made use of a manner that might without full knowledge of the circumstances have justified Bossuet's accusation of self-righteousness.

The Congregation of Cardinals continued their conferences until March, 1699, when Louis XIV urged the pope to a decision. The pope was torn in complying with the ultimatum of the king, since he held Fénelon in high esteem yet dared not set aside the pressure of a monarch. On March 12, 1699, the brief of condemnation was read in the little Chapel of Monte Cavallo before the Congregation and the pope signed it. The brief was reproduced immediately and appeared on all the principal news posts of Rome; it was sent by a fast messenger to Paris and in ten days' time it was in the hands of the king.

The Comte de Fénelon, in Paris at the time, carried the news to Cambrai, arriving on the Feast of the Annunciation as his brother was going into the pulpit. The archbishop remained alone for a little time then proceeded to the pulpit and preached *extempore* on "submission to authority." A few days later the official notification reached him. He called home the Abbé de Chanterac and immediately prepared his *mandement* and acceptance of the brief, much to the dismay of his enemies. As soon as the king gave him permission he published it. "At last our Holy Father has condemned this book, together with the twenty-three propositions extracted from it, in a brief dated March 12, 1699, which is spread abroad everywhere, and which you have already seen. We give our adhesion to this brief, both as regards the text of the book and the twenty-three propositions, simply, absolutely, and without a shadow of reserve . . ."

All the archbishops of France assembled their bishops to examine and accept the brief and all provincial assemblies were unanimous in condemnation of the *Maximes*.

D' Aguesseau has recorded Fénelon's ready submission as being a solitary case where no appeal was made for a retraction. "The credit of this is due to the wisdom and superiority of the mind of the archbishop of Cambrai, who was able to see that an over-great desire to justify one's self does more harm than good, and that the surest way to obliterate wrongs unjustly imputed is to let them be forgotten and die out in silence; while, furthermore, his knowledge of men must have taught him that he was likely always to be condemned by more than three-fourths of his judges, because there would always be a full three-quarters incapable of understanding him."

The conclusion of the controversy was no clear-cut victory for Bossuet, even though his nephew had at first shouted, "God is stronger than man; the truth has triumphed; the gates of hell have not prevailed against the church." The *Maximes* was prohibited and condemned because of twenty-three extracts, but it was not branded as heretical, nor was it ordered burned. Bossuet had charged Fénelon with a great crime and the College of Cardinals had decided he was guilty of a small one. Therefore, Bossuet was never satisfied with the submission that Fénelon seemingly made to the brief of the pope, and the completeness of the archbishop's outward acceptance of the order was made a reproach to him being called by his enemies "too dove-like." Whatever had been Fénelon's reaction to the decree, it is possible that Bossuet would have reacted as Master Whimsical in the *Fables*: "We must not be silent, we must not talk, we must not laugh, we must not be sad." At any rate he never dismissed the idea that Fénelon had attempted to set himself right at any costs in the eyes of Rome. "It was not thus that men recanted in the early church," he wrote. However, Fénelon's was not a heresy.

Baron von Hügel points out in that scholarly work *The*

Mystical Element of Religion that the very doctors and theologians who condemned the *Maximes* endorsed the same doctrines embodied in later pamphlets such as *Instruction Pastorale, Lettre sur la Charité* and *Lettre sur l' Oraison Passive*, "The doctrine intended by Fénelon in his *Maximes des Saints,* and as explained by him during his controversy with Bossuet, has never been censured, although the opposite party labored hard for its condemnation. Fifteen years after the condemnation of his book, we find him restating to Pope Clement XI [who as cardinal had drawn up the brief of his condemnation] in careful scholastic language the doctrine intended by himself, but which he himself had misstated in his popular treatise. As there were errors, the other side, whatever the crudity or novelty of some of its contentions, whatever its motives or methods—and some of them were far from creditable—was sure to succeed in the end. And it is well that it should have succeeded as far as it did succeed."

9

A Distance on the Road

Ah! must—
Designer infinite!—
Ah! must Thou char the wood ere Thou
    canst limn with it?
                              —Francis Thompson[1]

AN OLD engraving of *Cambrai* sets before us neat farm-houses and squared, orderly fields laid out on a vast and gently sloping hill crowned by the magnificent feudal castle and Gothic cathedral of Cambrai. Beyond lay sharp bluffs topped by the thirteenth-century citadel, with its heavy ramparts and sturdy buildings. Both cathedral and citadel overlook the Scheldt River. To Louis XIV this small unknown town was only a name that figured in his continuous frontier wars. Cambrai

---

[1] From *The Hound of Heaven*. Used by permission of Burns, Oates & Washbourne, Ltd.

had long been a center of war—fortified by Charlemagne, captured and pillaged by Normans, besieged by Hungarians, racked by three centuries of feudal warfare, and bartered ever since as a pawn among European powers, it bore the scars of violence and the poverty of its periodical devastations.

To Fénelon it was a far outpost from Versailles, where "all the affairs of the universe have their starting point and center." On the day of his nomination he wrote: "My life has been full of liberty and pleasantness, of congenial study and delightful friends. I am leaving them for a life of ceaseless slavery in a foreign land."

Cambrai was the ecclesiastical center of the Flemish provinces, conquered by Louis XIV in 1678. Half the diocese stretched beyond the frontiers of France. In the old days the archbishop of Cambrai had taken rank as one of the princes of the Holy Roman Empire and had been given sovereign rights over his diocese. His dominion included both Brussels and Antwerp and he set up his own fortress, garrison, and mint. The honors and powers of the archbishop had been reduced long before the Abbé de Fénelon took up his duties. And although he was given rank as Duke of France and a prince of the Holy Roman Empire, both titles were without the privileges once belonging to them. He did, however, become the largest landowner of the province with a revenue of one hundred thousand francs, provided it could be collected.

The palace of Cambrai was in keeping with the royal dignities of the office. To Fénelon, approaching it from the south, it presented a massiveness and magnificence not out of line with his former environment. Above its high walls were masses of buildings with many towers and steeples—mixed in architecture, Gothic and Renaissance. The lavish feudal palace, with its stables full of carriages and its ample halls and apartments with marble chimneypieces, polished floors and rich upholstery of crimson velvet fringed and garlanded with gold, was set down in the midst of Flemish simplicity and mediocrity. There was nothing French outside the palace gates—language, habits, modes of thought were strange to the new archbishop.

The Catholics of Cambrai expected an easy familiarity with their archbishop and were prepared to offer a warm and simple welcome to the noble from distant Périgord and Versailles. At first they did not feel at ease with his courtly manners and distinguished bearing, and their openness and lack of ceremony both amused him and ruffled his serenity. But in time he came to know their worth and to find "in this Flemish mediocrity people are both less good and less bad than in France; neither vice nor virtue goes so far; but the average man and young girl of the community is more straightforward and more innocent."

The crude little town of Cambrai in Flanders was far from the episcopal palace of Meaux in more ways than one. Fénelon, immersed in the duties of his diocese and Bossuet with his incessant movement between Versailles and Meaux, never found the road that ran between them, if ever they sought it. There was a rumor—never hinted at by the faithful Ledieu, who certainly would have recorded it—that on one occasion St. André was sent by Bossuet as a mediator.

After the papal condemnation of the *Maximes*, Bossuet, ever a valiant champion of the church, continued to be active in other controversies, although he never received a recognition commensurate for his services, an honor for which he half-hoped. The nuncio in Paris averred that Bossuet ought to be made a cardinal and sent to Rome, but neither Louis XIV nor Mme. de Maintenon made any effort in this direction. Ecclesiastical honors did not come his way although he stood far above his contemporary churchmen. He was too great and too powerful to be safely a member of the Roman See. His last two years were filled with great physical suffering to which his indomitable will refused to bend. Not only did he continue actively his pastoral duties, carried about on a litter, but he never ceased to translate the Psalms into French, writing and studying up to the very hour of his death. In the last hours friends gathered around him assuring him that his works would give him immortal fame. The dying man remarked, "Cease this discourse. Ask God for the forgiveness of my sins."

At Meaux today a small stone pavilion, built by Dominique de Ligny on the base of an old tower and surrounded by a little garden, is all that remains of the once dignified and delightful personal establishment of Jacques Bénigne Bossuet. The episcopal palace still offers a reminder of the splendor of the "booming France of Louis XIV." Gobelin tapestries line the walls of the great hall; beautiful marquetry tables adorn it. Centrally hangs the magnificent, masterful portrait of Bossuet by Rigaud. There stands the Eagle of Meaux in his purple and scarlet robes with all the grandeur of ermine cape and lace dalmatic, as though he would forever thunder forth the divinity of kings and the immutability of the status quo. The tides of war and the flux and flow of empire have passed before his unastonished eyes.

The room is redolent of the history of France. The bewildered Louis XVI and his courageous queen stopped here on June 24, 1791, on their disastrous flight to Varennes; here Napoleon Bonaparte took shelter three months before his surrender at Fontainebleau; in 1870 the German, von Moltke, sat in Bossuet's own chair; Charles X spent anxious hours in this old apartment. And it was from Meaux the taxicab army of Gallieni drove the German hordes from the Marne in 1914.

Immutable too—a word he favored—the handsome statue of Bossuet stands today in the Gardens of Meaux. It stands as did the living Bossuet solidly with considerable dignity and massive comeliness, allied with a grave and ingenious strength. A static quality pervades the man.

When the bishop of Meaux was gone, Mme. de Maisonfort wrote to Fénelon: "I used often to ask God to reunite you." Soon after Mme. Guyon's expulsion from Saint-Cyr, her cousin, Mme. de Maisonfort, had requested residence in the Visitation Convent in Meaux so that she could put herself under the direction of Jacques Bénigne Bossuet. Although in the years that followed she continued to have great respect and love for her former director, she was unable to communicate with him until after the death of the bishop of Meaux in 1704. She then wrote an account of Bossuet's last days and entrusted the letter to Ledieu to be delivered to the Archbishop of Cambrai—a mission eagerly accepted by the curious, note-taking little secretary of Bossuet. Never the less, it must have taken a stout heart, and

considerable self-confidence, as well as a strong portion of ordinary curiosity, to venture thus into the stronghold of the man
whom his master had succeeded, after years of bitter pursuit, in
disgracing—at least from the point of view of the court.

When Canon Ledieu arrived with the message he was given
a genuine Flemish welcome, good will was extended to him by
the household that had in five years grown up around its distinguished host. He was accorded the honors of the palace and
in his twenty-four hours of poking and prying about the prem-
ises he captured the surface life of Cambrai as accurately as he
might have done in a modern camera. His was not an un-
prejudiced mind, however, and his interpretations of what he
saw are not altogether accurate. Although he was officially
received by de Chanterac, his chief attention was fixed on the
tall, spare figure of the archbishop, who was now accustomed
to wearing the episcopal purple robes, but free of the gold and
lace usually worn by prelates. Fénelon received him graciously
and throughout the secretary's stay extended to him every careful courtesy within his power. On only one occasion did he refer
to affairs at Meaux, and that was to ask, "Who helped M. de
Meaux to die?" This question the complex minds of Saint-
Simon and Ledieu have twisted into an expression of guilt.

In his bold substantial script Ledieu set down a full picture
of every move and attitude his active eye detected. In his *Memoirs* he has sketched for us the scenes so that without effort we
can envisage the handsome room hung with crimson velvet
draperies adorned with golden fringes and galloon and set with
its marble mantels. We catch the gracious spirit of the prince
in purple robes acting as host to the secretary of his enemy:

A Distance on the Road

On arriving at the dining hall we found the other guests awaiting us, we washed our hands without ceremony, and the archbishop, taking the head of the table, said Grace. M. de Chanterac sat on his left hand, the rest of the party placed themselves indiscriminately, I taking a humble seat among them, and soup had already been handed round when the archbishop signed to me to take the vacant chair on his right. I objected that I was already served, but he politely insisted, so I obeyed him and changed my place, my soup being carried after me by a servant.

The dinner was very abundant and magnificently served, several soups, good beef and mutton, game of all sorts, splendid grapes and peaches, and excellent red wine; the bread was good, the table linen clean, and there was a great quantity of costly silver plate. There was a great array, also, of footmen in livery, who waited noiselessly and well; the butler was a man of very imposing appearance and seemed to be a great authority in the household.

. . . The Archbishop ate very little, and only of dishes very plainly dressed, in the evening nothing more than a few spoonfuls of eggs cooked in milk, with a glass or two of weak white wine—it is no wonder that he is so thin and pale. But for all his spareness, his complexion is clear and his health pretty good; though he had only that morning returned from a three weeks' visitation, he did not show the slightest sign of fatigue . . .

Fénelon conducted himself as bishop of Cambrai, Saint-Simon remarks, as though he always had been the bishop.

To Joseph Clement of Bavaria, a refugee to Cambrai, Fénelon wrote on the occasion of his friend's assuming the duties of the episcopate of Cologne, and in the letter is reflected his own high regard for his holy office:

The larger are the dioceses you have to control, the more extreme and pressing are their needs, so much the more will you require an apostolic courage, to be able to labour in them with much fruit. In fact, if you wish to be a Bishop, my lord, in the name of God, take care that you are not one by halves. . . . You must be meek and humble of heart, firm without haughtiness, and condescending without softness; you must be poor and mean in your own eyes, in the midst of all the nobility of your birth, from which you cannot of course separate yourself, but you must give to that nobility only as much as you cannot possibly refuse to it. . . . You must be a lover of sincere good advice, careful to seek out true merit and to be generous to it; finally, you must bear the Cross in contradictions and oppositions, and go to the ministry as if you were going to a real martyrdom.

O how much love is necessary, never to be discouraged, and always to bear patiently the crosses of this state of life! It is easy enough for those shepherds who only take care of the flocks for the sake of the wool and the milk; but it is terrible for those who devote themselves entirely to the salvation of souls. . . . It is prayer alone which can form a true Bishop in the midst of all these difficulties.

The business of the great diocese was efficiently handled even during the anxious years of Rome's deliberations. "I must confer with the chapter on a lawsuit; I must write and dispatch letters; I must examine accounts. How dreary would be life made up of these perplexing details but for the will of God which glorifies all he has given us to do."

Fénelon threw himself into the duties of his work, and, if at first it was "ceaseless slavery," he found it later to be his one source of consolation. With an energy of love astounding to his people and his clergy he won and kept his hold on the hearts of the Flemish people and with his usual suppleness of mind made his court a center of intellectual thought and genial exchange of lively wit. The people molded him, so to speak, as "water that takes on all color." By his intellectual power and imaginative personality he had been able to sway the Parisians, and at Cambrai he learned to speak from his heart. He no longer carried sermon notes to his pulpit but spoke with an engaging candor what spiritual truth the occasion demanded. At the same time he lived as a modest prince in his palace and as a village priest among his people. Simple and orderly living was the secret of his power and efficiency, for his austerity was in reality a purposeful and rationed expenditure rather than a self-conscious mortification. It represented the beauty of an orderly and clean mind that naturally turned away from gaudy gewgaws and the disorder of the unnecessary. His beautifully written manuscripts and letters testify to this quality within him. Saint-Simon reports on his nice balancing of things; "At the time of his death all M. Cambrai's affairs were in such perfect order that he neither owed nor left behind him a sou." And again it is seen in the request concerning his burial: it should be simple, he said, with the least possible expenditure of money—"this is not a mere conventional expression of humility, but because I think money laid out on funerals had better be kept for more useful purposes . . . and also I think the modesty of a bishop's funeral should set the example to the laity."

The archbishop knew every country curé of his diocese. His carriage drawn by three horses was a familiar equipage on the back roads of the whole province. Clothed in his fine violet episcopal robes, a book or a pencil in his white-gloved hands, and his long legs wrapped in a bearskin rug, he managed both the duties of his diocese and visits to the remote parishes year after year. He knew the temper of his priests, their poverty and their virtues, and their weaknesses too. He understood the "pardonable eccentricities" of the village parishes and handled them both delicately and firmly. He turned to training his priests whenever occasion presented itself—in retreats and on festival occasions, and in weekly conferences on the origins of religion. His gift with people helped him always. He listened with infinite patience to their problems. Ramsay wrote of this: "Often objections that they made were beside the mark. Far from impressing this upon them, he put himself upon the level of each one, suiting himself to their capacities, and giving weight to the feeblest dispute by some turn which made it possible to go to the root of it. I have often heard him hold these conferences, and have admired the apostolic humility with which he made himself all things to all men, as much as the grandeur of his discourse."

The French translation of the New Testament "Blessed are the meek" has a gayer lilt: Blessed are the debonair. They have a good bearing, a pleasant gallantry, an exchange of favor between gentlemen, a dignity in their giving. The debonair conducts himself with courtesy; he says, "Is there anything in the world I can do for you?" Fénelon's was a boundless charity during those twenty years' exile at Cambrai, whether the poverty of the suppliant was spiritual or material. He visited the peasants in their fields and accepted the hospitality of their homes; he carried medicines to the sick, and when they were dying, and within his reach, he himself sat with them to the end. When war came to Flanders he threw open the palace doors to officers, soldiers, and displaced persons on either side of the lines of creed and nation. Shelter and comfort were always to be found in his warm charity. Fénelon retained his gaiety and wit, his lively capacity for delightful conversation and ardent relationships with men and women of all ages and levels. He never stood aloof from life as an old man viewing with envy the oncoming generation. Rather, as he was letting go of old relationships he was reaching forward to the new generation and putting the impress of his personality on the future.

Children were always a part of his environment and with them he had an excellent rapport; they spoke a common language. Childlikeness, joyousness in life, was a fruit of the spirit that grew with him as the years came on. At the end of a long letter full of commissions to his nephew, de Beaumont, he observes, "There are five or six white rabbits beneath my window; they would make splendid rugs; but it would be a pity, for they are very pretty, and they eat like any great dignitary." Not a deadly seriousness, but joyful littleness was his frequent counsel to the stiff matrons who came to him for direction. "Make yourself little, madame, it is to children the kingdom of heaven belongs . . . woe to grown up people who do not make themselves little to resemble the little children." In spontaneous confidence he once wrote to Mme. Guyon: "I give my senses a little amusement. When I am alone I play like a little child, even in making oraison."

The suite of rooms over his state chamber, and the plain little bedroom in which he slept, was reserved for children, not only his own grandnephews but the children of his friends whose training he undertook as a part of his episcopal duties— though duty is not the word. "Mes vénérables marmots" he called them as they scampered in and out of the sober affairs of his diocese. The last brood to come under his care were the grandchildren of de Chévreuse, for whose parents the famous *Sur l'Education des Filles* had been prepared. "I delight in having them here, I love them dearly, they cheer me up and they do not trouble me in any way . . . [Of the oldest, Paul] I hope God will form him for the church. If he was a little older and I were a little less old I should have many schemes for him." He set them to work on the Greeks and Romans, using the same delightful methods of study and counsel that had been so effective with the Duke of Burgundy.

Fénelon had never lost contact with his former pupil, nor his hopes that through him he could effect a spiritual reformation of France. In 1711 Louis the dauphin, and the dauphiness, died, and the Duke of Burgundy became dauphin. With the advancement of the duke it appeared that Fénelon could be expected to return to Versailles, as chief adviser to the king-to-be. Louis XIV himself realized that his time was drawing to an end and placed into the hands of the young prince an increasing responsibility for affairs of state. Every move at Versailles that brought the Duke of Burgundy closer to reigning and toward the throne brought Fénelon nearer to political power. The court of Cambrai was as eagerly sought in those days as was that of Versailles.

The following year came a shattering blow. The new dauphin died, as did his wife and two of their three sons—some said of poison. Great was the consternation throughout the kingdom extending even to Ireland. Jonathan Swift noted the tragedy in his diary, commenting on the disaster that he oversaw overtaking France. When word came to Cambrai of the death of the young dauphiness, Fénelon wrote his old friend, the Duc de Beauvilliers: "For a long time I have had terrible fears for him; if God be no longer enraged against France, he will recover, but if the wrath of God be not appeased there is much to fear. I can ask nothing. I tremble and I cannot pray. . . . May the Lord pity us." The next day he wrote, "I begin to hope that Monseigneur le Dauphin will not die. . . . I have found it easy to pray for him. . . . Yet there is a fear at the bottom of my heart that God's anger against France is not appeased." Two days later the dauphin died.

And to his other friend, the Duc de Chévreuse: "Alas, mon bon duc, God has taken away from us all our hope for the church and for the state. He formed this young prince, he adorned him, he prepared him for the greatest enterprises; he showed him to the world and suddenly he destroyed him. I am seized with horror and overcome by prostration without any illness. While weeping for the dead prince who has torn the fibres of my heart, I am yet alarmed for the living."

Once again the natural resiliency of his spirit asserted itself. The child before whom he had set the challenge and obligation of kinghood in *Télémaque,* the youth who was to work a revolution in the hearts and lives of all Frenchmen, the Duke of Burgundy in whom his hope of power lay, might be dead, but there still remained the claim of the living.

As the years went by, Fénelon's lean figure became leaner, even while his spirit became more distinguished and purposeful. The common complaints of old age did not attack him—the dimness of mind, the ordinary illnesses of an aging body, the peevishness of spirit, all passed him by. His free soul was gradually loosening itself from the bondage of the body and the ageless part of him was continually and more easily responding to the challenge to perfection that never left him. His desire for it was as strong at sixty as at twenty.

"On the last day of Antony Watteau's visit we made a party to Cambrai," wrote Walter Pater, nearly two hundred years later. "We entered the Cathedral Church; it was the hour of vespers, and it happened that Monseigneur le Prince de Cambrai, the author of *Télémaque* was in the choir. He appears to be of great age, assists but rarely at the offices of religion, and is never to be seen in Paris; and Antony had much desired to behold him. Certainly it was worth while to have come so far only to see him, and hear him give out his pontifical blessing, in a voice feeble but of infinite sweetness, and with an inexpressibly graceful movement of the hands. A veritable *grand seigneur*. His refined old age, the impress of genius and honors, even his disappointments, concur with natural graces to make him seem too distinguished (a fitter word fails me) for this world. *Omnia vanitas!* he seems to say, yet with profound resignation, which makes the things most of us are so fondly occupied with look petty enough. *Omnia vanitas!* Is that indeed the proper comment on our lives, coming as it does in this case, from one who might have made his own all that life has to bestow? . . ." So did the archbishop of Cambrai in his later years appear to the sensitive historical imagination of Walter Pater, of the late nineteenth century.

A Distance on the Road

In this was his distinction There was multiplicity in his
life—literary, political, social, and ecclesiastical issues divided
his time and effort and interests, yet at no time was he tricked
into making them the end of his existence. As nesting birds use
all the odds and ends of twine and straw that come their way
to fulfill the basic instinct of their nature, so this gifted soul
used the events of his time to fulfill the basic drive of his being
towards God and thereby put his mark on history.

Fénelon's graciousness of spirit was never so superb as in
these latter days of his life and yet at no other period was he
more conscious of his own weakness. He had a sense of secret
faithlessness, since perfection stood beyond his human grasp.
"I feel the approach of old age and I am growing accustomed
to it without losing my hold on life; when I examine myself,
I seem as though I were in a dream, and I appear to myself
like a picture in a vision; I think I have no desire to taste of
the world; it seems as if there were a barrier between it and
me, which prevents any longing on my part, and which would,
I fancy, stand not a little in my way were I one day called upon
to return to it. There is a fundamental element of self-interest
and instability in me of which I am ashamed. The slightest
thing that saddens me makes me dejected, while the smallest
matter that pleases me a little, elates me beyond measure. Nothing is so humiliating as to be thus lenient toward oneself, and
hard on others, so cowardly at the sight of even the shadow of
a cross, and so prone to cast every burden off at the least glim-
mer of joy. But all is good. God opens a strange book before
us for instruction, when he makes us read our own hearts. I
am to myself as it were, the whole of a great diocese, more bur-

densome than the outside one, and a diocese which I am incapable of reforming."

To an aging man he wrote during these last years: "If we renounced every day of our lives, we should not have so much to renounce when it came to the last day, and that which terrified us at a distance would lose its terror when close at hand if we abstained from nourishing our dread with anxious speculations. To die daily will rob our final death of all its sharpness . . . M. Olier during his last days used to take up his own hand and say, Body of sin, thou wilt soon go to corruption; O Eternity, thou art very near me. It is not a question of rejoicing at the prospect of death; such joy does not depend on ourselves . . . Let us be satisfied with what does depend upon our own free will upheld and strengthened by grace. And this is; not to hearken to the promptings of nature, but to accept heartily that in which we are unable to rejoice. St. François de Sales distinguishes between consent and feeling. We are not masters of our own feeling but we are by God's grace masters of our consent."

The dissolution of his physical ties affected Fénelon less than the breaking up of his old relationships. The last two years of his life were marked by the deaths of four of the closest friends of his life—the Abbé de Langeron, the Duke of Burgundy, the ducs de Chévreuse and de Beauvilliers. To Mme. de Beauvilliers he wrote in August, 1714, just before his own death; "Let us unite our heart to him we mourn. He is not gone from us, because invisible; he sees us, feels us, loves us, is aware of our needs. Happily in port himself, he prays for us who are still exposed to shipwreck. He is forever calling us with an inner voice to hasten after him. All pure spirits see, hear and love their true friends in their common Centre. Their friendship is as mortal as its Source . . . A holy friendship only changes visible companionship for that of faith; it weeps but amid tears it is comforted by the hope of rejoining beloved ones in the home of truth; in the very heart of Love itself."

These are courageous and comforting words. The meaning of these friendships was made articulate in intimate letters to various correspondents of long standing. "I only live on friendship now," he said. "And friendship will be the cause of my death . . . One is tempted to wish all friends could arrange to die on the same day . . . or better still like Philemon and Baucis, one should become an oak when he sees the other changing into a poplar . . . People who love no one would be content to bury the whole human race with calm satisfaction and dry eyes . . . We shall soon find again those whom we really have not lost. Day by day we get nearer and nearer to them by rapid strides. It is we ourselves who are dying . . . I am sad but at peace . . . The heavy sorrows which we see coming grow familiar by degrees . . . The dead walnut trees are a sorrow to me."

His words seem almost a foreboding of the accident that occurred in November of the same year as he was returning from one of his pastoral visitations. His horses shied at a windmill and the carriage overturned. Although there was no serious difficulty at the time and he seemed to recover almost immediately from the shock, a relapse occurred a few weeks later. He wrote of the mishap to the Chevalier Destouches, his gourmet-friend, later in the month.

"A fairly long absence has delayed the answer which I owe you. It is true, my dear fellow, that I have been in the greatest danger; I am still uncertain how I escaped; no one was ever more lucky, although I lost three horses. All my servants shouted to me: 'All is lost, look out for yourself!' But I did not hear them at all, the windows being pulled up. I was reading a book, having my spectacles on my nose, my pencil in hand, and my legs in a bearskin rug; thus more or less was Archimedes situated when he perished in the taking of Syracuse. The comparison is absurd, but the accident was frightful. I shall always be a coward when I am on a bridge near a mill. You will notice, if you please, that the mill-wheel which touched one of the edges of the bridge without any hand-rail, suddenly began to turn the moment that we were passing; one of the pole-horses was afraid at a very awkward moment and threw us out on the side where he had no business to be; but dying himself he saved my life: for he stopped the carriage in a depression of the bridge which prevented my falling far . . ."

The letter goes on with friendly badinage, warning the chevalier that he would be wiser to wait until spring to make a visit to the northern country of Cambrai. "I am keeping you for a happier time of year; you must come with the charms of spring on the wings of soft breezes. You will see very soon two travellers with whom you may plan this trip. I should actually be especially glad to have them here when you come, to help me to entertain you, and to share in my pleasure . . . Goodnight,

my dear fellow; must I really believe you to be sober and wise?
I would give anything to believe this; but how in the world
can I be so credulous?"

The springtime visit never took place. The "Goodnight"
spoken to his genial friend was the last but one that Fénelon was
ever to express to the chevalier. A few weeks were all that were
left to him; fever and weakness ensued, rapidly growing more
severe throughout December and the first week of January,
1715. His period of illness was one of great serenity. He had
met extreme trials, as well as deep joy and high honor, he had
learned the dignity of self-control and suffered fellowship
with the dying. During the last week he would have no concern
brought to him except the reading of the scriptures and of
them he asked only for St. Paul—as though there was something of the ongoing vigorous spirit of this first missionary
that supplied a need in his own soul. "We walk by faith, not by
sight . . . We are confident and willing rather to be absent from
the body to be present with the Lord . . . Wherefore we labor,
that whether present or absent, we may be accepted of him."
He would ask that such a passage be read over and over again.

On Epiphany the shadows darkened perceptibly in the great
state room where he had been brought in the early days of his
illness. He lay surrounded by the grieving household, who
knelt beside him. When all the last things had been done, both
for the diocese and for his family, what hovered in his mind
as he waited for his release from the world that sometimes
seemed to him a puppet show of shadows which might vanish
at any moment? That moment was very close. One may well

François de Fénelon

believe it was a moment of ecstasy, when life, the underlying
total of consciousness, came into power; when all the accumulated richnesses of a lifetime were at his command; when
perceptions were clear and he was aware of an Other imping-
ing on his soul, an Other he had sought all his life. So far had
he gone—no small distance on the road. Death could well have
been the consummation of his one intention of being, as the
author of *The Cloud of Unknowing* put it, "the swift piercing
act, an act of direction, the naked intent of the will fastening
itself upon God." A short act in which is caught up "the
substance of all perfection . . . naught else but a good will, and
this good will the shortest work a man can imagine, for it is
neither longer or shorter than is an atom." The element of
Durée, the continuity, the flow of time, could well be the experience of dying, "In this uncertainty what am I? A something
that runs as rapidly as water, that dies in the same moment as
which it is born . . ."

"Lift the stone and you shall find Me; cleave the wood and
there am I . . ." In his life, as in the work of a poet, there has
sounded, dim sometimes but undeniable, a tone of beauty, a
cadence as of the chimes of infinity running, sometimes clear,
sometimes dimly, throughout the whole.

10

Director of Souls

S PIRITUAL direction," said Fénelon, "should be an intercourse of pure faith, all fidelity and death to self into which
nothing human may enter."

In nothing was Fénelon so much a master as in his spiritual
direction, for he had a sure insight into the various temperaments that passed under his care. He also had an artist's love
for his work, molding an ideal even while he let it shape itself
under his hand. In nothing was he so modern in practice and
theory. In the above description of spiritual direction he set
forth the necessity of objectivity and detachment through
transcendence of personal conflicts on the part of the director
as an essential for the fine art of counseling.

In much the same manner the modern counselor states the
ideal of his profession. He recognizes his vocation as an art—
he becomes the father-confessor, the interpreter, the guide, the

trainer even while he has a vivid participation in the inner
and outer conflicts and struggles of the other. While together
they enter into the deep forest of the inner world of the one,
wandering in an uncertain maze, the burden of certainty rests
on the director. He has confidence that if they are patient,
honest, and courageous enough they will in the end come to the
place where both are free and in harmony with the law of life.
Transference and countertransference, resistance and counter-
resistance, projection and counterprojection, are suffered by both,
but that which distinguishes the counselor from the counseled
and prevents his being drawn into the bogs that threaten to
drag down his companion is his own conscious and successful
transcendence of deep psychological problems. He has been, so
to speak, in the forest before, and is not only trained in the age-
old principles of the path but has had an experience by which
he helps the other to unmask, recognize, and come to terms
with his hidden self.

Paralleling this experience of modern psychological counselors
is that set down by the archbishop of Cambrai in a letter to his
niece, Mother Mary of the Ascension. The letter comes out of
twenty years of experience as a director of souls:

I hope, my dear niece, that God who has called you to rule over
your sisters, will take from you your own spirit, and will give you His,
that you may do His work. The work of God is to make Him loved, and
to destroy ourselves, that He alone may live in us. Your duty then is to
die to the natural man and love God. Ought you not to die, if you wish
to teach others to die? Ought you not to love, if you wish to inspire them
with love? No instruction is efficacious unless our example accom-
panies it. No authority is bearable unless example softens it. Begin then

by acting, and then you may speak. Action speaks and persuades; words alone are nothing but vanity. Be the least, the poorest, the most obedient, the most recollected, the most detached. . . .

Do not encourage any imperfection, but bear with all infirmities. Wait patiently for the souls that progress slowly; you run the risk of discouraging them altogether if you are impatient. The more need you have of strength, the more necessary it is that you should add to strength, sweetness, gentleness and consolation. . . . You must put yourself, by your condescending gentleness, at the feet of all those who have raised you above their heads. . . . Suffer; It is only through suffering that we learn how to compassionate others, and how to console them. . . .

Speak little, listen much; think much more how to understand the souls under your care, and how to meet all their needs, than of saying fine things of them. Show an open heart, and let each of your sisters find by experience that there is safety and consolation in opening her own heart to you. Avoid all severity; if correction is necessary, do it with kindness and discretion. Say nothing but what must be said; but say nothing except with sincerity and openness. Let no one fear that they may be deceived if they believe you. Be slow in deciding, but when once you have come to a decision, decide with firmness. Follow each one without losing sight of her; and run after her if she is escaping from you to remain apart from you. You must make yourself all things to all the children of God, that you may gain them all. Correct yourself that you may be able to correct others. Ask to be told of your faults, and believe that which is told you about those faults which your self love conceals from you. I am, my dear niece, full of zeal for you and devoted to all your interests in our Lord.

The modern counselor also has an invariable confidence in the law of growth—that the counseled must find himself as he can and no premature insight will assist. Inner truth is given to each seeker as he is able to cope with it. Each has his own way to find.

François de Fénelon

"Spiritual guides ought not to display all people's faults to them until such time as God prepares the way." So wrote Fénelon to the Père Lami in 1710. "They ought to watch a failing patiently, and say nothing until He begins to speak in inward rebuke. Sometimes even, it is necessary to imitate God's dealings with souls, who often so softens His rebuke that the person rebuked feels rather as though he were accusing himself than being accused. Anything like impatient reproof from being shocked at great faults becomes a very human correction, not that of grace. Our own imperfection makes us hasty to rebuke the imperfect; and it is a very subtle and all permeating self-love which cannot forgive the self-love of others. The stronger it is, the more critical the censor will be; there is nothing so irritating to a proud, self-willed mind as the self-will of a neighbor. . . . But he who is full of the love of God, is full of forbearance, consideration and indulgence. He waits and adapts himself and goes softly, one step at a time. . . . And so a wise spiritual guide will sometimes wait years to give a wholesome counsel."

However, he did not tolerate spiritual sloth or dependence on him as a director. For, as Aldous Huxley comments in *The Perennial Philosophy,* "A letter from the Archbishop of Cambrai—what an event, what a signal honour! And yet it must have been with a certain trepidation that one broke the emblazoned seal. To ask for advice and a frank opinion of oneself from a man who combines the character of a saint with the talents of a Marcel Proust, is to ask for the severest kind of shock to one's self esteem. And duly, in the most exquisitely lucid prose, the shock would be administered—and, along with the shock, the spiritual antidote to its excruciating consequences. Fénelon never hesitated to disintegrate a correspondent's complacent ego; but the disintegration was always performed with a view to reintegration on a higher, non-egotistic level."

The charm and power of Fénelon's spiritual letters have never waned. They are read and reread, for in them he has captured that which is perennial and common in the spiritual gropings of each man and woman. The proud, the intellectual, the religious and the atheist, and the insecure and the emotional are not confined to any one era. They are all faced with the same hard mountain to climb until, emancipated, they can take their places on the heights where the meaning and relationship of spirit and earth are manifest.

All the superficiality of seventeenth-century France, all that is fascinating and unique in its fine arts and court life, all that is stimulating in its philosophical, political, and ecclesiastical controversies may be spread out before us in detail as in a vast landscape painting displayed in a museum. To the intelligent observer the outspread scene has value and meaning as he sees it in relation to that which has preceded and that which is to follow; but even so it remains remote from his experience. This is not the case with Fénelon's spiritual letters. Here is a series of little masterpieces. They seem to be created specifically for each one who chances upon them; and through them, wherever or whenever he lives, he becomes the recipient of a wisdom that transcends space and time. Their author had ac-

quired a detachment that lifted him above such limits. It is as if
he wrote himself out into the infinite that is the summation of
all, so that anyone with sufficient desire to reach into the eternal
finds his hands filled with still-living words.

Although these letters speak to the heart they are not without
intellectual integrity because the writer had a well-trained,
analytical mind; he had been disciplined by teachers who gave
no quarter in developing dialectic; he showed profound regard
for the process of reason. But there is a point at which
reason is left behind and mind wings its way with the sureness
of instinct, as if the spirit were a great bird on its flight to its
nesting-grounds. Sometimes Fénelon passes within hailing distance of that deep-seeing earlier author of *The Cloud of Unknowing* who likewise laid aside his "fullhead of knowing"
and in humility acknowledged, "I would leave all that thing
that I can think, and choose me to love that thing that I cannot
think. For why; He may be well loved, but not thought. By love
may He be gotten and holden; but by thought never." Fénelon
never abused his own knowledge of the world, neither of nature
nor of affairs; he merely laid it aside as a swimmer might lay
aside a garment which was useful in its time but contributed
nothing but weight to one who was struggling in deep water
against a strong current.

"Why reject so many lights that console the heart," he said to
the philosopher Chevalier de Ramsay, "because they are mingled
with shadows which humiliate the mind? Should not true religion both elevate and cast down the man—show him, at the
same time, his grandeur and his feebleness? You have not yet

a sufficiently comprehensive idea of Christianity. It is not only
a holy law, which purifies the heart; it is also a mysterious
wisdom which conquers the spirit. It is a continual sacrifice
of our entire self in homage to the Supreme reason. In prac-
tising its morality we renounce pleasures for the love of the
Supreme Beauty. In believing its mysteries we immolate our
ideas out of respect for eternal truth. Without this double
sacrifice—of thoughts and of passions—the holocaust is imperfect, our victim is defective. It is by this sacrifice that the entire
man disappears and vanishes before the Being of beings. . . .
The Infinite Being ought to be incomprehensible to the creature.
On one side is seen the Lawgiver, whose law is entirely divine,
who proves his mission by miraculous facts, which cannot be
doubted—by reasons as strong as those which we have to believe them; on the other we find mysteries which shock us.
What is to be done between these embarrassing extremes, of a
clear Revelation and an incomprehensible obscurity? We find no
resource other than the sacrifice of the mind; and this sacrifice is a part of the worship of the Supreme Being. . . . Restrain
then, your imagination; silence your reason; say, without ceasing, to God: Instruct me by the heart, and not by the mind;
cause me to love as the saints have loved. By that you will be
safe from all fanaticism and incredulity."

Fidelity to little things marks these letters. The voluble de
Chévreuse poured out all his experiences and in his letters
gout and Jansenism, educational theories, and mortgages jostled
together with his state of soul. Fénelon sorted out all his concerns one by one and gave to each its appropriate attention,

and then suggested how the overworked duke might manage the multiplicity of life. "You waste too much time on everything, you are not slow, but you fly rapidly from one thing to another, and yet let each one carry you too far. Sobriety is what you chiefly need, sobriety of thought and language, and that is only to be gained by prayer: you should proclaim a solemn fast from argument and cut things short from morn to night."

Love of little things and perfection in them was, he said, the nature of God himself. "God exhausts Himself to find a strayed lamb. God appears in the little events of life. . . . and it is in small affairs that our love of Him may be manifest . . . The great virtues are rare, the occasion for them seldom comes. The small occasions are unexpected. They return every moment. They place us constantly at odds with our pride, our idleness, our scorn, our quickness and our chagrin. . . . We should a hundred times rather make some sacrifices to God, however violent and painful, on condition that we be freed with liberty to follow our tastes and habits in every little detail. It is, however, only by faithfulness in little things that the grace of true love sustains us, and distinguishes itself from the passing favours of human nature. . . . But the most dangerous thing is that the soul, by the neglect of little things, becomes accustomed to unfaithfulness. . . . Thus it is not by fussiness that we become faithful and exact in the smallest things. It is by a feeling of love which is free from the reflections and fears of the anxious and scrupulous. We are carried away by the love of God."

Yet exactitude and attention to small events segments life and imprisons the individual in the affairs of time. He describes his ideal: "It seems desirable to me that you should combine great exactitude with great liberty. The first will cause you to be faithful, the latter courageous. If you aim at being exact without freedom you will fall into scruples and bondage; if, on the other hand, you affect freedom without exactness unduly, you will yield to laxness and negligence."

". . . This liberty of soul which gazes immediately before it as it goes forward, but loses no time in reasoning about the steps, studying them, constantly considering those which it already has made, this is true simplicity. . . . I have often noticed that the world has the same liking that God has for a noble simplicity which forgets self. . . . The true simplicity seems sometimes a little careless and more irregular, but it has a feeling for frankness and truth which makes us conscious of a certain openness, gentleness, innocence, gaiety and serenity which is charming when we see it near-to and continually, with pure eyes." Indeed, these are the very traits which those who lived near to the Archbishop of Cambrai in his last years point out in him over and over. His austerity was gentle, his humor kindly, his charm unfeigned, his joy as quick as his kindness and both encompassing and free to all. Never realizing that he himself had it, he apostrophizes, 'O, how amiable this simplicity is! Who will give it to me? I leave all for this. It is the pearl of the Gospel. O, what will it give those who want it only.' "

There is a Scottish work, very short, entitled *Advice and Consolation for a Person in Distress,* that was inspired in its publication by the great success of Ramsay's *Travels of Cyrus,* a near relative to *Télémaque.* It contains vivid phrases like the above: "Who will reach out his hand to help you out of the mire? Will it be you? Ha! 'Tis you yourself who are sunk into it, and cannot get out, besides this mire is yourself. The whole source of your misfortune is you cannot get out of yourself."

The letters are directed to all types of men and women in all degrees of spiritual growth from a *gourmet,* Destouches, to an ascetic monk, Père Lami. One unusual instance of spiritual direction is that of Chevalier de Ramsay. He came to Cambrai in 1710, when twenty-four years of age, and stayed six months. He later lived for years at Blois in the household of Madame Guyon. During his time at Cambrai, de Ramsay recorded his *Spiritual Conversations* with the archbishop.

It is a long way from the dark wynds of Edinburgh to the open plaisances of the episcopal palace at Cambrai; but Ramsay not only bridged this gap most successfully but also the greater distance from the harsh Presbyterian doctrines of the Covenanting baker who was his father to the troubled and fervent Catholicism of Fénelon. Through devious, if always scrupulous, ways this cosmopolitan gentleman and distinguished philosopher made his way across Europe, through the mazes and doubts of a hesitating deism, to a faith that satisfied his sensitive soul. He discovered as well a personality to which he clung, which he loved, revered, and studied to excellent effect. His biography of the archbishop of Cambrai is still valuable and informative.

Ramsay had spent three years at the University of Edinburgh where he became particularly interested in mathematics and theology. He also acquired strong antiquarian interests, and developed a feeling for the classics. Of a sensitive and overscrupulous nature, his was the type of mind most prey to adolescent doubts; Ramsay became at this time a deist. Through the trial of a Scottish clergyman who had upheld the "pernicious views" of Antoinette Bourignon, the Flemish mystic, Ramsay became involved in the general study of mysticism; thus his mind was prepared for the further studies awaiting him on the Continent. His enthusiasm for Newton also was marked.

Through one or more officers who had served in the Low Countries during the War of the Spanish Succession, Ramsay secured the means of getting in touch with Fénelon. What he heard of the former preceptor to the Duke of Burgundy fascinated this eager and searching mind. He made his way to Cambrai and there became one of the circle of international figures of distinction who gathered about Fénelon. Fénelon's hospitality was expandable, as were his concern and energy. So amid the affairs of diocese and state, he found time for long conversations in which he "examined religion" with a young man eager for truth. They discovered, or thought that they did, that there was no middle course between deism and Catholicism. Fénelon disposed of the non-Catholic sects with a statement that their tenets depended on their members' reliance on their own feeble individual judgment; the Catholic Church, however, provided for human weakness and instability. Ramsay at first jibed at the idea of reliance on the institution of the Catholic Church, and brought up the question of the frequent cases of corruption among priests of all religions. When Fénelon answered these doubts in rather vague general terms, the doubter retired and begged for time to consider these problems. He now became, as he has told us, very much depressed. "My spirit enveloped itself in heavy clouds. I felt all the attacks of incredulity." He wished to depart from Cambrai and momentarily went so far as to distrust his host's integrity.

Ramsay was no shallow youth setting out to the Continent to wind up his education in the fashionable style, with a smattering of pictures, cathedrals, salons, and gaming halls. The urge that took him to Europe in the first place seems to have been the result of deep religious unrest; he was seeking, as he said when he set out for Leyden, the *summum bonum* of existence. However, he wisely decided to submit these questions frankly to Fénelon and, obtaining a private interview, he knelt down before the archbishop and related his difficulties. The problem of the condemnation of Fénelon's book *Les Maximes des Saints*, troubled him; he felt that if Fénelon accepted his condemnation, as he seemed to be doing with resignation, he must be a hypocrite, since he necessarily must believe the tenets he had set forth. Fénelon met this with a reasonable refutation, however, stating that the ideas he had set forth in the *Maximes* were not wrong in themselves, nor had they been condemned as such by the church; they had merely been unsuitably expressed in his book, which was one of dogma. "My book was worth nothing. I had not made out a case. It was the abortion of my mind and not the fruit of Grace in my heart. It is not worth your perusal."

These sentences have the ring of truth. Ramsay was now completely convinced of Fénelon's integrity. Fénelon had learned when to approach, when to retreat, when to leave the hesitating soul alone to meditate, to become mellowed in the essences of the teachings he had so eloquently and persuasively expounded. This recalcitrant spirit—and Ramsay was no easy prize—was allowed leisure for reflection, for his state of mind to coagulate, to "set," as it were, before further undertakings were made. One feels that Ramsay, in his scholarly and learned turn of mind, seriously wanted to believe; the battle was more than half won. The aging archbishop of Cambrai and the young scholar did not give up the battle until the last resource of reason was surrendered and the seeker no longer wished to possess the Truth but let himself "be possessed by Truth, taken captive and despoiled of false riches."

Letters directed to one person over a period of time seem to lead forward by gradual steps, indicating that each letter had found its appropriate response. In them is revealed the constancy of the author, his concern, patience, and wisdom. In them the director is seen at work. Fénelon is the skilled gardener, coming into a garden in which the seed has already taken root. It was not in his power to make the seed grow, nor could he change its nature. He cultivated and enriched the soil, he pruned unbalanced shoots, and drove down supporting stakes.

One such series was directed to the Comtesse de Gramont. The countess was of noble Scottish family, having been born Elizabeth Hamilton, the daughter of George Lord Hamilton. She was married to the Comte Philibert de Gramont, who brought her from her native England to the sophisticated French court. "La belle Hamilton" was both before and after her marriage one of the shining ornaments of the court of Charles II. She was a woman of exceptional beauty, much sought after by the noblest and most renowned gentlemen of the kingdom. Her husband also belonged to a distinguished family. Although twenty years older than Elizabeth, he possessed much charm and wit. He had lived a life of great indulgence, and even when he dictated his *Memoirs* at the age of eighty was incurably frivolous. In the *Memoirs* her brother inserted a description of the countess: "She had the finest shape, loveliest neck and the most beautiful arms in the world; forehead white, open and smooth, nose small, delicate and retroussé. . . . She possessed an admirable discernment in distinguishing between the solid and the false. Her sentiments were noble and even lofty when there was occasion." The concern she had for spiritual counsel was sincere, and her relationship to Fénelon gave evidence of that basic integrity to which her brother referred. In a letter marked Paris, June 11th (no year), Fénelon spoke to his correspondent Elizabeth Hamilton de Gramont of the dangers of her prominent position in the social world. The world smiled on her and the most flattering portion of that world showed her its consideration. However, he told her frankly, she had definite faults, to wit: a taste for luxury, a haughty and scornful spirit, and frivolous habits of long standing. All this put together was, says the director, like a torrent which "carries you away despite your best resolutions."

Another letter suggests Fénelon's primary teaching and ideal of simplicity: he who had centered himself and all his acts in God was freed from artificial and self-conscious manipulations. He took neither a lofty nor a humble pose but could be himself in every society. "Perfect meekness is a true knowing and feeling of one's self as he truly is" was the common teaching of the saints. Meaningless formality and deadening artificiality were obnoxious weeds which Fénelon was uprooting. He restated the same ideal in his next letter, which was called forth by some formality of Elizabeth de Gramont in approaching him. "Your discretions, madame, are absurd. When you wish me to have the honor of seeing you, you have only to give me your orders. Simple and natural behavior is too pleasing to God to shock those who wish to serve him, and who should in his name recommend simplicity. So be simple in all things, madame, and simple in sending for me, as in all the rest."

A month or two later, after Fénelon had taken up his duties as preceptor to the Duke of Burgundy, he apparently was in closer touch with the spiritual difficulties of the countess. He wrote her a long letter of meticulous direction about her devotional practices, for he observed she was "letting her soul be used up by the court," reminding her that each duty had an appropriate place, and the duty of salvation had first place. "Consider then, madame, saving a half hour, mornings and evenings. By pretending to wake up later in the morning, and in the evening by having some letter to write, you can get away, and your real duties will be done no less well. Also you must take advantage of every odd moment, when you are waiting for someone, when you go from one place to another, when you are with people whose talk runs on, so that all you need to do is to let them talk, you can lift your heart to God for a moment, and by so doing refresh yourself in the midst of your activities. The less time one has, the more important it is to manage it. If a person waits to have regular and convenient hours by himself, in order to fill them with serious things, he runs the risk of waiting too long, especially in the kind of life which you lead; but one must take advantage of every broken moment. The life of prayer is continuous, it is not a scheduled affair as is the world's business. . . . In one moment we can recall the presence of God, love him, adore him, offer him what we are doing or what we are suffering, and in his presence calm all the agitation of our hearts. . . . As for your faults, they are harder to bear; but they turn to our advantage if we use them to humble ourselves, without relaxing our efforts to correct ourselves. Never did a person need more urgently to be humiliated by her faults than you do. Only thus will God crush your pride and confound your intellectual conceit. When God has taken away all your resources, he will build his own edifice. Until then, he will demolish everything by your own faults. Allow him to do this. Work humbly without counting on anything."

Fénelon, like Mme. de Maintenon and Mme. de Sévigné, was not unaware of the countess's unlovely and harsh attitudes toward those who disrupted her plans. He attacked her asocial behavior with his customary sureness and gentleness. He reminded her that God concealed himself behind these irritating persons and the more troublesome they were the more effectively they served to break the stubborn will. Her impatience with people seems to have been a besetting weakness with which she struggled for many years. Four years later he wrote again: "Madame, you always have to endure both other people and yourself. If you only had to endure others, and if you had never experienced in yourself any of the wretchedness which you condemn in the other person, the poor neighbor would seem to you a monster to be exterminated. But God allows you to have much to endure from your haughty, unfair, and rebellious temperament, so that you may learn to bear all the provoking qualities in imperfect people . . ."

Yet again he wrote her on the subject of human relationships: "I have only one thing to say to you about love of your neighbor. Only humility will soften you in that respect. Only the sight of your own wretchedness can make you sympathetic and tolerant towards that of another. You will say to me, I can see that humility will help me bear with my neighbor but what will give me humility? Two things put together will produce it. Never separate them. The first is the view of the abyss of misery from which the powerful hand of God has drawn you and over which he still holds you as though suspended in air. The second is the presence of God who is all. It is only in looking steadfastly at God, and in loving him, that we forget ourselves, that we free ourselves from this bauble which has dazzled us, and that we become accustomed to finding refuge in our smallness under the lofty majesty which engulfs everything. Love God and you no longer will love yourself. Love God and you will love all that he wishes you to love for him of him . . . As the light increases, we find ourselves more corrupt than we thought. We are astonished at our former blindness, and we see emerge from the bottom of our hearts, as from a dark corner, a myriad of shameful snakes. We should never have dreamed that we carried such things in our breasts, and we feel a horror of ourselves, as we see them emerge. We must neither be astonished nor discouraged. It is not that we are more wicked than we were. On the contrary we are less so. But as our sins diminish, the light which shows them to us waxes brighter and we are seized with horror. But remember, for your comfort, that we only notice our sins when we are be-ginning to be cured of them."

Here is an echo of that unknown director of fifteenth-century England who sought to bring a young man along the dangerous road from self to God. "Wonderfully is a man's disposition changed by feeling within his spirit this nothing nowhere wrought. At first when a soul looks upon it, he finds there all the particular sins he has ever committed since he was born—both in body and spirit. Each one is separately and darkly painted upon it and wherever he turns they will appear before his eyes until there comes a time—a time of hard travail, sore sighing and woeful weeping. Then they are washed away."

Like his anonymous predecessor, Fénelon counseled the Comtesse de Gramont to "look on this nothing nowhere wrought," to wait in silence, for in such meditation and intro-spection was healing of soul to be had. The process through which he was going paralleled the work of integration of personality in every age. A clear analogy is apparent here with

[232]

the methods of the psychiatrist of today. Out of a dark and dull complacency she was thrust into the chaos of change in order to make a creative adjustment on a higher spiritual level, where new and sensitive vision enabled her to see the demons lying in the valley of her soul. In the silence of reflective moments they rose up from the unconscious. "But do not worry about them," he said, "you are seeing them and getting rid of them. It is by acknowledging them that they will cease to trouble you. This is the way to spiritual perfection."

At this stage Mme. de Gramont seemed in a state of constant irritability and uncertainty, brought on through an analytical consideration of her former life. Then, too, the affairs of court seemed altogether out of harmony with the ideals she was beginning to appreciate and desire. In participating in such a pattern of living she felt guilty of all sorts of infidelity. Her inclination was to cut herself off from her former associates. Her director was sympathetic at this point for he too was weary of the superficiality of such life and had similar temptations, yet he was very sure that such a course was wrong.

He wrote her from Versailles: "You are afraid, madame, of being unfaithful to God in your duties, and you are right. Nothing so blocks grace as a sluggish soul, which, by wanting freedom, refuses to God what it feels he demands, or else delays. However, we must also avoid falling into over-scrupulousness. Consider, simply, then on every occasion what true courtesy demands . . . You must be strictly fair in this. However, you should not break off too completely from the pleasures of worldly chatter."

[233]

This was the beginning of a long period of scrupulosity. "A scrupulous man teases God, irritates his neighbor, torments himself, and oppresses his director," wrote Father Faber, another wise director of souls. It is a false sort of righteousness by which insecure souls seek to satisfy themselves, thinking they are as holy as they are miserable. To one suffering from this anxiety, Fénelon wrote after years of counseling: "This heart of mine is much oppressed and weary for you . . . Oh, what I would not give to be able to cure you." Abandonment to the will of God is his continual counsel. He has no other answer for anxiety. He would teach her to pray as he himself prayed: "Lord, I know not what to ask of thee. Thou only knowest what I need. Thou lovest me better than I know how to love myself—Father, give to thy child that which he knows not how to ask. Smite or heal, depress me or raise me up: I adore all thy purposes without knowing them, I am silent; I offer myself up in a sacrifice; I yield myself to Thee; I would have no other desire than to accomplish thy will. Teach me to pray. Pray Thyself in me."

I shall have difficulty, madame, in remembering the things which I said to you last Sunday. All that I have kept in mind, it seems to me, is that I told you two things. First, that we ought to sacrifice ourselves in the state that Providence has placed us, without making plans or patterns of virtue for the future; and second, that we ought to have a very great faithfulness to God in the smallest things.

Most people pass the better part of their life in knowing and regretting their manner of living, in proposing to change it, in making rules for free time which they hope to have and which often is not given to them, and thus in losing in resolutions the time which they ought to be using to perform good deeds, and to work profitably towards their salvation. . . .

Our salvation is the task of every day and every moment of our life. There is no better time to work for it than that which God gives us now, in His mercy, because we have today, and perhaps we shall have no tomorrow. Salvation does not come by wishing for it, but by working for it with all the best in us. The uncertainty in which we live ought to make us realize that our will should be centered on this one concern, and that every other occupation is unworthy of us, since it does not lead us to God who should be the end of all our actions, and who is the God of our salvation. . . .

To watch oneself is to be attentive to God. It is to have Him always present. It is to withdraw into oneself. It is not to be weakened or distracted willingly among His creatures. It is to love as much as we can the retreat, the holy books and prayer. It is to expand, as the Prophet said, one's heart in the presence of God. It is to find Him in one's self. It is to seek Him by the fervor of one's desires. It is to love Him more than all things, and to avoid all that we know is displeasing to Him. This virtue, madame, is the virtue of every state. It is a wonderful relief at court, and I know nothing which can help us more not to love the world, in the midst of the world, than the use which we know how to make of this virtue.

The importunities of the world should detach you from yourself. Bear in peace this constant burden and you will not cease to advance in the narrow way. It is narrow because of the pain which wrings the heart, but it is large because of the stretch which God gives to the heart from within. We suffer, we are surrounded by adversity, we are deprived of even spiritual consolations; but we are free, because we want everything which we have, and we should not want to be released from it. We endure our own weakness, and we prefer it to the most pleasant circumstances, because it is God's choice. The great point is to suffer without being discouraged.

As a member of a great Catholic Scottish family the Countess had close contact and sympathy with the cause of the Cavaliers

in the fighting in Ireland. One brother was involved. During
1690 Fénelon wrote her many letters of sympathy both in regard
to the cause dear to her heart and for the misfortunes that over-
took her brother. "We must adore His purposes without understanding them. . . . God has tried you by the things that are
happening to your brother but He only tries you to make you
more worthy of Him."

Some of the most poignant letters drawn from the spiritual
correspondence of directors such as de Sales, Fénelon, Caussade,
Dom Chapman, von Hügel, have set forth the use of suffering
as a means to spiritual growth. The soul can be made to stride
when the body rests. After sympathetic encouragement to
health, Fénelon wrote Mme. de Gramont, who was enduring a
trying and disfiguring illness: "How happy we are when we
suffer, provided that we really wish to suffer and to satisfy the
justice of God! What do we not owe to him, and what pain
we should strictly deserve! An eternity of torment changed
into a few rashes! . . . These are the graces which a heart
must feel which has been touched by the goodness of God. Had
he covered you with leprosy he still would spare you. The
leprosy of pride, of sin and of self-worship, were much more
horrible. It is from this that he has cured you. I cannot wait,
madame, to ask you at Fontainebleau how you are getting along
in the penitence and the retreat in which God has placed you.
Those which we choose are nothing. Only God knows how to
crucify." Strong medicine indeed.

By September the lady has somewhat recovered, so that there
was a prospect of her returning to Fontainebleau, where Féne-

lon evidently had his residence as preceptor to the Duke of
Burgundy during this period. He spoke of freedom. "This free
situation is only a beautiful idea. Perhaps we shall never attain
it, and we must keep ourselves ready to die in the servitude of
our state, if Providence prevents our plan of retreat. You are
not your own, and God only asks of you that which depends on
yourself . . ."

Throughout the correspondence there are frequent references
made to friendly meetings about the marble fireplace where
deep searchings, as well as lighter moods, found expression;
there is frequent mention of the friends who centered around the
Hôtel de Beauvilliers; as well as gracious and kindly concern
for each other's health. In the latter period of their correspondence Fénelon changed from the pronoun "you" to "we," and
the comradeship of the spiritual way became more apparent.
The friendship was no surface affair and was unchanged by
the disgrace that removed Fénelon from the social circle at
court. His last letter from Versailles to Mme. de Gramont at
Bourbon expressed a weariness with court life that she must
well have appreciated: "Versailles does not rejuvenate me this
way [as does Bourbon]. Here one must have a smiling face, but
the heart smiles but little.

"However little remains of personal desires and sensibilities,
there is always something to watch out for here. No one has
what he wants. He has what he would rather not have. He is
grieved over his bad luck, and sometimes over the good luck of
others. He despises the people with whom he spends his time

and curries their favor. He is bothered, and he would be very upset not to be and to live in solitude. There are a swarm of little hovering cares, which come every morning as you wake, and which do not leave you again until evening. They come in relays to annoy you. The more a person is in favor, the more he is at the mercy of these imps. This is what is called life in the world, and the object of envy of fools. However, these fools are the whole blind human race. Every man who does not know God who is all, and the nothingness of all the rest, is one of those fools who admire and envy a very unhappy state. The sage also has said that the number of fools is infinite. I hope with all my heart, madame, that you have the good spirit which God gives. . . . This remedy, which heals the heart, is preferable to the waters which heal the body . . . This is too long a sermon. Forgive it, please, to a man who has long kept silence." And a last letter of appreciation for the loyalty she accorded him before he left court permanently: "I cannot end, madame, without begging you to tell the Comte de Gramont that I shall never in my life forget that he did not blush for me, and that he acknowledged me without embarrassment before the courtiers at Marly. . . . It is only you, madame, who will not receive any compliment from me. I content myself with wishing you a heart humbled under the hand of God and softened towards your neighbor, a mind simple as a dove and wise as a serpent, to avoid everything which can corrupt you; finally a true detachment from the world and from yourself, the practice of which may be real and constant. All goes well with us, when we go forward in this way, because it is the one and only way for us. Success, reputation, favor, talent, comforts are only delusions."

Of more importance perhaps than the de Gramont letters are those directed to Mme. de Montbéron, wife of the governor of Cambrai. Her only claim to fame is being the recipient of letters that continue to speak to anxious souls. These letters, written after Fénelon left court, are marked by an informality not found in the earlier ones. Every rule of religious living may be found in them as well as intimate little paragraphs about his own spiritual state. Fénelon was not deceived when he undertook the responsibility of directing Mme. de Montbéron—her very difficulties inspired him to give her the best counsel of which he was capable, a carefulness and skill that have caused this series of letters to be ranked among the best of their kind. He spared no pains to offer her that secure relationship through which she might be able to find her way to the freedom of an integrated life. Although the outcome of this long struggle is uncertain, many facts militated against him. She was a woman past middle age, her noble birth and high official position had bound her to a chafing traditional pattern. She was proud and intelligent. Her two grown children were married, and without this concern she had time for introspection. In middle life the emotional instability rooted in her childhood—as Fénelon told her—increased, and made her perpetually unhappy and fearful. The modern counselor would say that psychological problems of late life are intertwined with religious difficulties and religious problems have a psychological base. Carl C. Jung gives as his experience: "Among all my patients in the second half of life . . . there has not been one whose problem in the last resort was not that of finding a religious outlook on life. It is safe to say every one of them fell ill because he had lost that which living religions of every age have given to their followers, and none of them has been really healed who did not regain this religious outlook." By religion he did not mean the institutional church, but the reaching out of the deep soul of man for his eternal relationship with God. Fénelon states this condition when he assumed officially the responsibility of giving her direction. In it he not only pointed out her insecurities and disillusioned her about her behavior, but sought to establish himself as a companion and almost a champion as they entered into the business of releasing her from her fears:

You have two things, madame, which support one another, and are the cause of infinite harm to you. One is your scrupulousness, which has been rooted in your childhood, and carried to the last extremities during so many years; and the other is your attachment to relishing and feeling what is good. Scruples often take from you the enjoyment and feeling of love, by the trouble into which they throw you. On the other hand, the cessation of this enjoyment and feeling awakens and redoubles all your scruples; for you think you are doing nothing, that you have lost God, and are a prey to delusion, as soon as ever you cease to relish and feel the fervor of love.

. . . You have passed your whole life in believing that you were always devoted to others, and never to yourself . . . You love yourself so much that you always wish to take credit to yourself for not loving yourself at all; all your consideration for others only goes far enough to make you fear you may not be sufficiently satisfied with yourself; this is the root of all your scruples. You may discover the depth of it by your tranquility about the faults of others. If you regarded God alone, and His glory, you would be as sensitive and as acute about the faults of others as about your own faults. But it is the *I* which makes you so sensitive and so acute about these last. You wish that God, as well as man, should be pleased with you and that you should always be pleased with yourself for all you are doing for God.

. . . Here you have, madame, the vanity and corruption which God wishes to show you deep down within your heart. You must look at it with the peace and tranquility that constitute true humility . . . Your sensitiveness that seems so right, leads to wrong; nothing prevents you so much from being simple, and even from being candid; it makes you guilty of deceit and double-dealing, of which you are scarcely conscious yourself. As soon as you feel you are losing your simplicity and peace, tell me of it. If you cannot speak to me, at least tell me that you cannot, in order that I may break the ice in spite of you, and exorcise the dumb devil.

. . . Moreover, I must tell you once for all, in the presence of our Lord, Who sees the inmost recesses of conscience, what you never have been willing to believe up to this time, but what I have never ceased to assure you of: and that is, that I have never felt up to this present moment, either repugnance, or disgust, or coldness, or difficulty about anything with regard to you . . . I have thought and still think that your sensitiveness in taking everything upon yourself and hiding your troubles from him who ought to know them causes you to be guilty of reserves, which others are guilty of through falsehood . . .

He told her that the venom of self-love must be openly dealt with so that the heart might be emptied of it. "You would never otherwise have been thoroughly able to know it. For myself, far from being tired of you, and of the care of leading you to God, I am only tired of your discreet reserve. My only fear is lest I may come to have this fatigue, which you imagine me to have now.

[241]

"But you shall not escape me; I will pursue you unrelentingly, and I hope that God will make you see, after the storm has abated, how much affection I have for you, for His glory . . . Unite yourself with me before God, to let Him accomplish in you that which rebellious nature fears. Distrust not only your imagination, but also your intellect and the ideas which seem to you to be most clear. For myself, I am going to pray unceasingly for you; but I do so with a feeling of bitterness and a suffering of soul which is worse than a fever. I beg of you . . . not to give up obedience. I am waiting for you and nothing shall console me except your return."

So began a relationship that extended over some fourteen years during which time Mme. de Montbéron began the long process of spiritual growth.

The letters that contain the deepest wisdom came out of the later period of life, when Fénelon had been tempered by the disaster that isolated him from court. The life of love and prayer is the leading theme of these letters, which offer counsel on every imaginable problem that could confront the sincere seeker after truth.

In them one can trace also the spiritual journey of the writer, for often his own struggle is reflected and his own experience related. He had a persistent passion to become humble and simple. Abbé Dimnet, referring to the beauty of his delicate spirits shortly before he died, remarks: "Fénelon was a high-strung person. Had he not patiently counteracted it with spiritual exercises he would not have left behind him a memory which everybody respects. He was by birth and disposition an ambitious man aiming at the highest posts of church and state. In the banishment of Cambrai he might have brooded on injustice and died in bitterness instead of developing the exquisite gentleness for which he was famous. Soul culture saved him."

11

Temporal Affairs

A MYSTERIOUS charm diffuses certain personalities, which causes them to glow in an unearthly light and appear alien to mundane affairs. Such a one-sided point of view veils the true force of character and falsifies the purity of its principles—principles that seem too fragile to be tested in the violent affairs of men. This misfortune has befallen Fénelon at the hands of some of his biographers. An exceedingly inaccurate idea of the *doux* Fénelon has prevailed for many years. Francis Thompson, writing on mysticism, refers to him as a "pastor of courtly sheep" and Evelyn Underhill calls him a "perfect gentleman talking to perfect ladies." This scarcely portrays a man who dared to tell Louis XIV that his whole kingdom had become one vast hospital, and one who could administer a sound rebuke to the Duke of Burgundy for his lack of soldierly conduct, nor does it chime with the courage with which he took

up the unpopular cause of interior prayer even though it involved him in personal disgrace.

It would be an endless task to penetrate into all the involve-
ments of Fénelonian criticism, as through the years scholars
and historians have contributed each his own quota to the
legend. Sharp witticisms have been exchanged; hits that one
would have thought deadly have found their mark. The first
Life, that by Ramsay, is acute, interesting, and intensely admir-
ing and reverent, as would naturally be the tribute of an affec-
tionate friend and convert; but it gives little personal detail
and omits much that one might have expected to hear. The
volumes of L. Crouslé have been unanimously considered
spoiled by bitter ill-nature and prejudice. In 1808 appeared the
official Catholic biography by a loyal Sulpician, Cardinal de
Bausset, putting the approval of the church on Fénelon's reputation. Onésime Douen attacked the idea of the tolerance of
Fénelon in his book *L'Intolérance de Fénelon.* Thomas Upham,
writing his life of Mme. Guyon in America in the mid-nine-
teenth century, gives a stilted, out-of-date, and entirely un-
critical picture. Jules Lemaître has given a neutral picture in
his *Ten Lectures on Fénelon.* Lord St. Cyres, writing fifty years
ago, emphasizes in his well-written biography the worldly
side of the prelate; his picture of the liberal Catholic churchman is valuable. Paul Janet and P. M. Masson have contributed
charming, sympathetic, shorter studies.

The disciple and interpreter par excellence of Fénelon is the
Abbé Bremond. Henri Bremond has dug deeper and longer
than anyone else into the sometimes full, sometimes sordid

tangles of the chronicles of the great controversy. In his works on Fénelon, Abbé Bremond sets forth two profiles as delicate as drawings by Watteau, *Apologie pour Fénelon* and *Les Plus Belles Pages de Fénelon.* There is also the picture of Fénelon given in his *Le Procès des Mystiques.* Du Bos, who comments upon Bremond, feels that in the mind of Bremond "accompanying and almost traducing the theocentrist like a muted accompaniment of Mozart that almost gives the lie to the main theme" runs a strain of skepticism. He implies that Bremond has skirted only the edges of holiness in his study of Fénelon; nevertheless, in the depths of the changing souls of these two men there was a certain identity. The word of Du Bos himself for Fénelon is: "A poor forlorn figure and one never understood."

Masson says of Fénelon, "We too find him great—he who had enough richness and liberty of spirit to formulate the *Maximes,* look for holiness behind Mme. Guyon, dream of *Télémaque,* fashion the 'conscience of a king,' be a familiar of St. François de Sales and of St. John of the Cross, weep for La Fontaine and understand Molière."

Of particular interest are several books written since World War II about Fénelon: those by Gabriel Joppin and Ely Carcassonne are particularly valuable in indicating the trends of modern thought in regard to Fénelon. Carcassonne has especially emphasized the interpenetration of ideas coming from the Far East into European religious thought by means of the Jesuit missionaries in the seventeenth century.

Temporal Affairs

Fénelon's was an independent, reforming spirit by nature. He loved liberty as ardently as he did integrity and charity, and he considered all three as essential to the affairs of state as to the personal affairs of the soul. Therefore, he could not stand aloof from the political and social scene. His participation in secular affairs is not to be overlooked if the man is to be seen in the fullness of his personality. He was a convinced and eager protagonist of governmental reform. Not only did he formulate a political, social, and economic theory, but he also had high aspirations of initiating a spiritual revolution through the Duke of Burgundy. If the young prince had come to power and his mentor's revolutionary policy been adopted, this subtle and upright priest might have accomplished in France the reforms effected in England during the next century without a violent revolution.

Everything in his ideal state was to be regulated, given its appropriate status, even while he maintained that individual liberty was essential. Political systems are created to avoid the two colossal blunders of the state—arbitrary power and anarchy. "Anarchy is the height of evils only because it is the extreme of despotism . . . the medium is written law, always the same and sanctioned by the whole nation, which shall be above everything." Equally evil, then, was royal regimentation and revolutionary measures. The people in the end were responsible for affairs of state.

In his *Letter to the King,* and later in *Examination of Conscience for a King* and the *Tables of Chaulnes,* he censured a monarch who would plunge a people into war or any other major operation that they themselves did not sanction. In addition to the monarch and the aristocracy there should be provided a parliament of the people. Justice was to govern the relationship between classes. The poor were not to eke out an existence in order to produce luxurious and useless articles for the aristocracy and the wealthy. Rather, all people were to live simply and the articles produced by the poor were to be those which contributed to the well-being of all. Fashions in clothing and styles of architecture for public and private building were to be governed by utility and natural beauty. Every family was to hold in perpetuity sufficient land for its needs—and when the country was overpopulated younger people were to migrate to sparsely settled parts of the world. Free trade was an essential factor in maintaining world peace and brotherhood. "O that all men held all things in common," he remarked to Ramsay.

Fénelon conceived the state as a scene for spiritual action and was convinced that the power of religion could lift a nation out of static misery into the creative purpose for which it was intended. However, the transformation could not take place en masse, but through a realization of individual vocation—in the acceptance by each citizen of his responsibility as a human being. Social progress, he maintained, as did Bergson one hundred and fifty years later, is dependent upon *somebody* —a personality—who has been courageous enough to venture beyond the limitations of time and space and, within the limitless realm of truth, discover and bring back into the static morality of the period the dynamic of a new and high ideal. Such a person possesses the power to call forth the idealism slumbering in the hearts of those who of themselves dare not venture so far. This *somebody* becomes the bearer of a cause that is larger than personal comfort; he is the actualizer of invisible truth for which men are willing to risk their lives. Faith and power are stirred anew and people are given the strength to take a decisive stride forward to a higher existence.

There was in existence, although latent, a brotherhood of man based upon the pure principle of God within every individual. "Men in all climates and all ages are bound together to a certain immovable Center which holds them united by certain invariables," he says. This unity of humanity in God was one of the inviolable laws, the denial of which by either nation or individual resulted in inevitable disaster. Would that I might have only been his body-servant so that I might have finally come to be his steward," cries Rousseau, who was moved in his hysterical manner to tears by the mention of Fénelon's name. The Fénelon who had written *Télémaque,* with its humanitarian idealism, spoke more strongly to the distressed and seething populace of this period than did the Fénelon whose spiritual directions revealed the mystical roots from which humanitarian virtue springs.

Liberty, the power to choose—rather, the obligation to choose—was a right of every individual and could not, without danger, be dissipated by a despotic government, he maintained. The expression of it was essential both to the individual and to the society in which he lived. Yet in all his writings about liberty he admits the sovereignty of the people only as a dire result of a monarch's inadequacy, in which case a reversal

François de Fénelon

of sovereignty is essential. "A sudden and violent revolution will come, which far from moderating the king's excessive authority will overthrow it beyond remedy," he predicts.

He was convinced that a hierarchy and a monarchy were essential, yet never was aristocracy to be a privilege; rather, it was a responsibility. "The gods did not make him a king for himself," he tells the young duke through *Télémaque,* "but that he might belong to the people; all his time, all his care, all his love is due to the people, and he is only worthy of royalty insomuch as he forgets himself to devote himself to the public good."

Fénelon belongs definitely to the group of utopian socialists —in the general and not the specific sense—such as Thomas More and Campanella. Henry Payne said of him that he was the most modern of the men of the seventeenth century. Yet his political and social theories did not materially affect the course of history in spite of their eighteenth-century popularity and endorsement by Rousseau. In their general and timeless breadth of view, as applied to the past as well as to the present political scene, they have much interest for modern-day liberals. Fénelon might have been a great statesman but that was not his vocation. All that he has said about affairs of state had been said in principle by men whose business was statesmanship. But the great value of his political theories is to show the extraordinary, farsighted, and wide view of the author himself as allied to the principles by which the mystics believe the world can be saved. His was one more clear voice to be added to that chorus of prophets who have spoken forth from the time of Moses and have kept alive the fundamental truths by which the human race continues to exist.

The same judgment may be set upon his status in the field of letters. Fénelon's literary work was secondary to his higher vocation. He was accepted as an authority in the literary controversy of the day between the Ancients and Moderns. His writings had given him recognition in the French Academy of Letters as early as 1693. A few months before his death he wrote one of his best works in the form of a *Letter to Members of the Academy*. This letter ranks with *Traité sur l'éducation des Filles and Télémaque*, as highest among his definitive literary achievements; but the center of his thought is to be found in his letters, as was that of Voltaire in his correspondence. His talent showed itself to the greatest advantage in his social circle, or to those who leaned upon him for practical advice in the planning of their lives. By the middle of the eighteenth century many of his works had been translated into German and English and were widely circulated. Even in far-off Philadelphia an unknown Quaker woman recorded in her Journal of 1756: "Fénelon's works appear on the parlor tables of the best educated." In fact, as early as 1725 his writings were collected and edited by Friends in England and America.

In the field of letters his tendency was to move away from the rigid standards that dominated his period into the expanding experimentation of the eighteenth century. He loved wide horizons, he reveled in the sweeping lines that symbolized the flow of eternity. His style has a fluid grace, in places soft and alien to modern taste, in other places ringing with hammering blows. Truth for him could not be blocked off into any one era; tradition and innovation were both valid in his scheme so long as they served the purpose of Truth; the good is in the old and in the new. As in his political theory he found in the framework of the old aristocracy an expression for limitless human responsibility, and as in his religious conceptions he gave scope for endless spiritual development within the boundaries of the formal church, so in literature and art he was willing to risk the conventional in old, natural and classic forms —"the simplicity of the dawning world," he called them. He had little use for the Romantics, comparing them to a Gothic cathedral, all windows, tracery, and pretentious artifice, insubstantial "like cardboard." "But true good taste eschews these meretricious glories. Our poems should be wholly free and simple, yet gracious and majestic, patterned on those stately Doric temples where there is no superfluous ornament . . ." Language and poetry and art were to be freed from bondage to rules and pretentiousness. He deplored systems of rhyme and patterns of verse that had made poetry a "discipline of useless torture." Prim decorum and powdered elegance were to be forgotten; instead, poetry was to flow freely and simply for everyone, for both the learned and the unlearned. "Nothing on earth is bettered by rarity; the beautiful thing does not lose but gains in beauty as it is made accessible to the whole human race." Panegyrics he considered as inappropriate as emerald crosses. "So many flashes dazzle me. I love a gentle light that refreshes my weak eyes. I choose an agreeable poet who adapts himself to common capacities; who does everything for their sakes; and nothing for his own. I would have a sublime so familiar, so sweet and so simple that at first every reader would be apt to think he could easily have hit on it himself; though very few are really capable of it. I prefer what is amiable to what is surprising and wonderful. I would have a man that makes me forget he is an author; and seems to converse with me upon the level." After life and movement Fénelon asks for order and clearness, both of which he says are to be labored over until they perfectly but unobtrusively sustain the idea. In literature and in art also he disapproved of regimentation and of anarchy.

As Francis Thompson says, there are in every age two currents of writing, the surface current and the undercurrent. The former represents what the age produces, the other shows what it develops. "The leaf does not fall from the bough until it has prepared the germ of the future leaf; an age does not end until it has prepared and enunciated the ideas which are to govern the succeeding age. This is its real contribution to the progress of thought, and this is the work of the writers who belong to the undercurrent." These words, written in relation to Montaigne, are equally true of Fénelon. He was indeed a sort of man who was novel in the seventeenth century, but the type of man who could speak to the coming century.

Fénelon's popularity among metaphysical philosophers extended well into the eighteenth century, as did his political and literary vogue. Thomas Reid, that eighteenth-century Scottish reactionary against the materialistic interpretations of Hume and Locke, placed high value on the philosophical work of the archbishop of Cambrai, *The Treatise on the Existence of God,* saying, "Fénelon's interpretation of the criterium of Descartes is the most intelligible and most favorable I have come across." In this volume Fénelon gathered up his philosophy on the nature of God, the universe, and man himself. Earlier, in his youthful experiences with the young philosophers who circled around Bossuet, he had produced something similar in refutation of Malebranche. This later and more complete text was not published until two years after his death. His arguments, based on Descartes, are far from modern but they continue to breathe forth clear impressions of faith and represent his acute and orderly type of thinking. There is in the work a warmth and a personal touch that makes it pleasant reading in spite of its obsolete development of ideas. After the minute examination of nature and the universe, from art he deduces the Artist and the meaningfulness of the whole, he is moved to consider himself—the I. Here he finds both the art and the Artist—the Planner planning through himself. Deep in himself *a priori* are the footprints of the Divine, which constitute the "grandeur of me." He calls these traces infinity, unity, and a law of righteousness—all of them so much a part of himself that he mistakes them for himself; but beyond these, and lending force and creative power, he discovers the will and its God-given volition to goodness.

"I find in my nature a something instinctive which is absolutely real, something which is in me; which is above me, yet which is in me even when I do not know it; something with which I am alone even as though it were myself, which is truly nearer to me than myself. This something so near, so wonderful, yet impossible to understand, must needs be God. . . . There is a principle which is pure, placed in the human mind, which in different places and ages hath had different names; it is, however, pure and proceeds from God. It is deep and inward, confined to no forms, nor excluded from any man when the heart stands in perfect sincerity." These are the words of John Woolman of whom John Greenleaf Whittier remarked, "Fénelon from his bishop's palace and Woolman from his tailor's shop in New Jersey speak to us in the same language." This experiential knowledge of the indwelling Light is the deepest truth of all religion, and in Fénelon's pursuit of it lies his continuing message for all time. It is the essential simplicity of his outward complexity.

One is reminded here of Mme. Guyon's famous analogy of water. A pure soul resembles water. "Since water is fluid and yielding, it assumes the form of the vessel in which it is placed. It takes on every form, every taste and every hue, but in essence is always the same."

Fénelon's sense of the rightness of things, or relevancy, operated in all his activity. He had faith in the appropriateness of created forms to the divine design, so that the mundane events in earthly affairs had meaning for him. He assumed a relatedness and an interrelatedness between things that made up an ever-enlarging and eternally forming design. There were no accidents and each event was a part of the flow of life, just as a drop of water falling from the sky to the mountain stream is in the ongoing flux of the river to the ocean from which and to which it is forever moving. The world was a phase—"a vale of soul-making," as Keats expresses it—with a relevancy to the eternal purpose.

"There is a natural design, a concatenation, by which all is brought with order to the superior cause. . . . It often happens that that which seems a defect to our limited understandings, in some separate and distinct part of the work is really an ornament with respect to the general design, which we are not able to survey with views sufficiently extensive and, at the same time sufficiently simple, to comprehend the whole. . . . If the characters we use in writing were of immense magnitude, every character at close view would take up the whole compass of man's sight; so it would be impossible to see more than one at once. . . . It is just the same with the large strokes of Providence, which it forms in the conduct of the whole world during the long procession of the ages. There is nothing intelligible but the whole—and that whole is too vast to be comprehended in a close view; when we at last come to the consummation of the ages, we shall see in God, that is, with a true point of view, the total of human events, from the first to the last day of created nature together with their proportions in regard to the design of God, we shall then cry out with transport, 'Lord, thou alone art just and wise!' "

Fénelon as a political theorist, literary critic, and metaphysician has always held a certain small place in the minds of men who are students of the period, but Fénelon the seeker of the innate wisdom of the soul continues to speak in vivid words to sensitive seeking hearts of all time. The mystical stream that flowed through his spirit continues to touch lives within and without the Catholic Church. It was an element in the intense and deep religious awakenings that also characterized the next century—including early Methodism, the Society of Friends, and various pietistic movements all over the Continent.

There is evident today a resurgence of a deep spiritual searching similar to that which presaged the spiritual revivals that marked the eighteenth century. Once again Fénelon's pursuit of the Infinite and his direction of the way to perfection is finding a response among the religiously alert. His letters are becoming a spur to holy living.

By his still-living words men and women are set on the path of love—a love from which all selfishness is to be purged, a love that is to love for the sake of love alone. By his ability to trust where he did not know Fénelon inspires to faith—a faith that is an intense assent to God's ordering of affairs as they are to be. By his prayer of abandonment to the will of God he leads them toward pure prayer—a prayer in which the soul meets God, where all the earthly part of himself is hushed so that the eternal presence may flow in and bathe the soul in the renewing flood of goodness.

As a spring of water from the mountainside is both old and new, so is the truth of Fénelon. With each generation he becomes a new expression of the cosmic purpose—the essential nature of life—the part that would find its appropriateness in the whole. He could say with St. John of the Cross:

Yet, if on the common land,
No longer am I seen or found,
Thou wilt say that I am lost:
That wandering, enthralled by love,
Myself I lost, and was found.

Table of Dates

1689-1695 Preceptor to grandson
of King Louis XIV,
the Duke of Bur-
gundy

1694 Commission of Issy   1694 Birth of Voltaire

1695-1715 *Archbishop* of Cambrai

1697 Banished to Diocese of
Cambrai

1699 Condemnation by Pope Innocent XII of Fénelon's
book, *Les Maximes des*
Saints.   1704 Death of Bossuet

1711 Jansenist stronghold of Port-
Royal destroyed

1711 Death of Dauphin (father
of the Duke of Bur-
gundy.)

1712 Deaths of Duke of Burgundy and of Duchess and
one child

Birth of Jean Jacques Rousseau

1714 Congress of Baden

1715 Dies at Cambrai, Jan. 7   1715 Death of Louis XIV

Bibliography

BAUSSET, L. M. F. *Vie de Fénelon* (Official Catholic Life). Giguet & Michaud, Paris, 1809.

BENNETT, CHARLES A. *A Philosophical Study of Mysticism*, An Essay. Yale Press, 1923.

BENSON, A. C., and TATHAM, H. F. W. "Men of Might," Edwin Arnold, Publishers to India Office.

BERGSON, HENRI. "Les Deux Sources de la Morale et de la Religion." Felix Alcan, Paris, 1934.

BERTAULD, PHILIPPE. *Bossuet Intime*, Desclée de Bouvier et Cie. Paris-Bruges, 1927.

BREMOND, ABBÉ HENRI. *Le Procès des Mystiques, Histoire Littéraire du Sentiment Religieux en France*, Tome LI. Librairie Bloud et Gay, Paris, 1933.

———. *Apologie pour Fénelon.* Librairie Académique, Paris, 1910.

BROWNE, SIR THOMAS. *Religio Medici.*

BRUNETIERE, FERDINAND. *Histoire de la Littérature Française Classique*, Vol. II. Librairie Ch. Delagrave, Pâris.

CARCASSONNE, ELY. *Fénelon, l'Homme et l'Oeuvre—Le Livre de l'Étudiant.* Boivin et Cie, Paris, 1946.

CHAPMAN, DOM JOHN. *Spiritual Letters.* Sheed & Ward, London, 1935.

CHEREL, A. *Fénelon, Lettres et Opuscules Inédites.* (Complement de ses Oeuvres et de sa Correspondance.) Librairie Hochstetter, Paris, 1917.

DRUMMOND, J. "A Candle in England—The Shadow of the Purple, Bossuet." Duckworth, London, 1947.

EDMAN, IRWIN. *Philospher's Quest.*

ELIOT, T. S. *Selected Essays.* Faber & Faber, Ltd., London, 1932.

Bibliography

FÉNELON, FRANÇOIS DE SALIGNAC DE LA MOTHE. *Works.* Edition Lefevre & Pourrat Frères, Paris, 1858.

——. *Works,* Édition Lebel, Paris, 1821-1830.

——. *Original Holograph Letters.* Morgan Library, New York.

——. *Selections from Fénelon.* Roberts Brothers, Boston, 1893 (Wisdom Series).

——. *Spiritual Letters* (translated by M. W. Stillman; edited by Rev. C. F. Whiston). Idlewild Press, Cornwall, N. Y., 1945.

——. *Christian Perfection* (translated by M. W. Stillman; edited by Rev. C. F. Whiston). Harper, New York, 1947.

——. *Advice and Consolation for a Person in Distress and Dejection of Mind with some Thoughts on the Remedys of Dissipation wrote for the Use of a Friend.* R. & A. Fowler, Glasgow, 1750.

——. *A Demonstration of the Existence of God.* R. Urie, Glasgow, 1744.

——. *Conversations with M. de Ramsai* (translated by A. E. Silliman), London, 1879.

——. *Spiritual Letters* (translated by Abbe Gosselin), London, 1892.

GRAHAM, REV. GEORGE. *Telemachus, A Mask.* Printed by A. Millar, London, 1768.

GUERARD, ALBERT. *Life and Death of an Ideal.* Charles Scribner's Sons, New York, 1928.

GUIZOT, M. *History of France,* Vol. 4. T. Y. Crowell, New York City.

GUYON, J. M. B. DE LA MOTTE. *La Vie écrite par Elle-Même.* Libraires Associés, Paris, 1791.

——. *Autobiography.* London, 1897.

——. *A Method of Prayer.* London, 1902.

——. *Torrents.* London, 1899.

HAMILTON, ANTHONY. *Gramont Memoirs* (translated by P. Quennell; edited by C. Hartman). Rutledge and Sons, London, 1930.

HAZARD, PAUL. *La Crise de la Conscience Européenne.* Boivin et Cie, Paris, 1935.

VON HÜGEL, BARON FREDERICK. *Mystical Element in Religion.* London, 1927.

Bibliography

HUTCHINSON, FRANCES E. *Henry Vaughan*. Clarendon Press, Oxford, 1947.

HUXLEY, ALDOUS. *The Perennial Philosophy*. Harper, New York, 1945.

INGE, W. R. *Christian Mysticism*. Methuen & Co., London, 1899.

JANET, PAUL. *Fénelon*. Librairie Hachette (les Grands Écrivains), Paris.

JOPPIN, GABRIEL. *Fénelon et la Mystique du Pur Amour*. University of Bordeaux, 1938. Gabriel Duchesne et Fils, Paris.

LANDOR, WALTER SAVAGE. "Imaginary Conversations" (Queen Elizabeth, Cecil, Duke of Anjou, Fénelon). J. M. Dent, London.

LANSON, GUSTAVE. "L'Art de la Prose." Librairie des Annales, Paris, 1909.

LAVEDAN, HENRI DE. "La Vie Courante (Le Prieur de Carennac)." Paris, 1909.

LAVISSE, E. *Histoire de la France,* Tome VII. Librairie Hachette, Paris, 1911.

LEAR, H. L. P. *Fénelon, Archbishop of Cambrai*. Longmans, New York.

LEMAÎTRE, JULES. *Fénelon, Dix Conferences*. Arthème Fayard, Paris, 1910.

———. "Le Mariage de Télémaque." Illustration Théatrale, June 18, 1910.

LEUBA, JAMES H. *The Psychology of Religious Mysticism*. Harcourt Brace, New York; Keegan Paul, London, 1925.

MARTIN, HENRI. *History of France*. Boston, 1865.

MASSON, MAURICE. *Fénelon et Mme. Guyon*. Librairie Hachette, Paris, 1907.

MASSON, P. M. "Oeuvres et Matières, Une Apologie pour Fénelon." Librairie Académique, Paris, 1923.

MAY, J. LEWIS. Fénelon, Archbishop of Cambrai. Burns, Oates and Washbourne, Publishers to the Holy See. ·

MURRAY, J. M. "Countries of the Mind—J. B. Bossuet." Oxford University Press, 1931.

PASCAL, BLAISE. *The Living Thought of Pascal* (Introduction by F. Mauriac). Longmans, 1940.

Bibliography

PATER, WALTER. "A Prince of Court Painters (Antoine Watteau)." (Imaginary Portraits.) Macmillan, London, 1910.

PEERS, ALLISON. *Spanish Mysticism.* Methuen, London, 1924.

RAMSAY, ANDREW MICHAEL. *Life of Fénelon.* J. & R. Parlane, Paisley, Scotland, 1897.

ROUMAGNAC, ROGER, and ANDRIEU, PIERRE. *La France—Paris et les Provinces.* Ode, Paris.

ST. CYRES, VISCOUNT. *François de Fénelon.* E. P. Dutton, New York; Methuen, London.

SCHAMONI, W. *The Faces of the Saints* (translated by A. Freemantle). Pantheon, 1947.

SEILLIÈRE, ERNEST. *Le Peril Mystique dans l'Inspiration des Démocraties Contemporaines.* La Renaissance du Livre, 1918.

SHELLEY, MARY W. and OTHERS. "The Most Eminent French Writers—Fénelon." Lea and Blanchard, Philadelphia.

SISTER FELICIA, O. S. A. *Seven Spanish Mystics.* Press of St. John the Evangelist, Shea Brothers, Cambridge, Mass.

SWIFT, JONATHAN. *Journal to Stella* (edited by Harold Williams). Clarendon Press, Oxford, 1948.

TAILLANDIER, MME. ST-R. *La Jeunesse du Grand Roi.* Librairie Plon, Paris, 1945.

THOMPSON, FRANCIS. "Literary Criticisms—Fénelon" (discovered and collected by T. L. Connolly, S.J.), Dutton, New York, 1948.

TILLEY, ARTHUR. *The Decline of the Age of Louis XIV.* Cambridge University Press (England), 1929.

UNDERHILL, EVELYN. *Mysticism.* Methuen, London, 1911.

UPHAM, THOMAS C. *Life and Religious Opinions and Experiences of Mme. de La Motte Guyon.* Harper, New York.

WILLIAMSON, C. O. W. "Great Catholics—Fénelon." Nicholson & Watson, Ltd., London, 1938.

ZERMATI, J. DAVID. "Fénelon, L'Économiste." Université d'Alger, 1947.
———. "Les Religieuses de Cambrai." First published 1793, Paris. Probably edition of 1797, since it contains the *Discours Preliminaire.* No title page (in Boston Athenaeum Library copy).

Index

Index

Index

Index

220-21, 224, 225, 226, 248; made
Archbishop of Cambrai, 177-78; at
Cambrai, 196-97, 200-1, 202-6, 223,
225, 242-43; last illness and death,
211-14; posthumous reputation, 244-
246; approval of Church officially
stated, 245; influence on 18th century, 249-51, 253-54; literary qualities and tastes, 251-53; essential
message, 253-58; writings, *see
Dialogue Concerning Eloquence;
Dialogues of the Dead; Epiphany
Sermon before the Siamese Ambassadors; Examination of Conscience
for a King; Fables; Letter to the
King; Letter to Members of the
Academy; Maxims of the Saints;
Pamphlets, misc.; Refutation of
Malebranche's Treatise on Nature
and Grace; Reply to Bossuet; Sermon on the Consecration of the
Elector of Cologne; Tables of
Chaulnes; Télémaque; Treatise on
the Education of Girls; Treatise on
the Existence of God*
Fénelon, Louise de La Cropte d'Arbe
(mother of François), 4; influence
of character on son, 5-6
Fénelon, Marquis de (uncle of François), 7, 8, 9; François member of
household of, 21
Fénelon, Pons de Salignac de (father
of François), 4
Fitch, William; *see* Canfield, Benoît
de
Fleury, Abbé, 27, 41, 54, 79
Fontainebleau, 72, 84, 137, 236-37
Fox, George, 129
François de Sales, St., 35, 104, 116,
123, 177, 187, 210, 236, 246; influence of Mme. Acarie, 105; and
Jeanne de Chantal, 125, 170; influence on Fénelon, 35, 125, 126-27;
influence on Mme. Guyon, 137;
writings, *see Treatise on the Love
of God*

"Friends of God" community, 114
Friends, Religious Society of; *see*
Quakerism and Quakers
Frost, Bede, 122

Gallicanism, controversy with ultra-
montanism, 93, 94, 95, 148; *see also*
Bossuet and Gallicanism
Geneva, Switzerland: Mme. Guyon in,
143; expelled from, 144
Germigny, 26, 27, 54
Gobelin, Abbé, 38
Godet des Marais, Paul, Bishop of
Chartres, 166, 168, 175, 187
Gosselin, on Mme. Guyon, 182
Gothic ornament, Fénelon's view of,
61, 252
Gramont, Elizabeth, Countess of
(born Elizabeth Hamilton), 227-28;
Fénelon's letters of spiritual coun-
sel to, 227, 228-39
Gramont, Philibert, Count of, 227-28;
Memoirs, 228
Grenoble, Mme. Guyon in, 143, 144
Guide to True Peace, A (Quaker
handbook), 182
Guyon family, 138, 139, 140
Guyon, Jeanne Marie de la Motte-,
93, 104, 129, 136, 149, 180-81, 191,
245, 246; early life and influences,
137; marriage, 137-41; development toward quietism, 137, 138-42
passim, 143-44; conversion experience, 140-42; and ecclesiastical authority, 144, 145, 171-73; Commission and Articles of Issy, 175-77,
178; imprisonment at Vincennes,
179; in Bastille, 182; and Bossuet,
169-73, 174, 175, 178, 180, 182,
183, 185; influence exerted by, 144,
146, 148, 159, 160, 167, 169; and
Mme. de Maintenon, 146-47, 148,
159, 167, 168, 169, 179, 186; and
Fénelon: first meeting, 148-53; important letters from, 135-36, 154-
158, 159, 160-61, 162-63, 168, 169,

Index

Index

temporary religious controversies in general, 31, 94 (*Declaration of the Four Articles*), 95, 96, 100; relation to Mme. Guyon and the quietist controversy, 144-45, 187, 189, 190, 191-92
Lourdes, incarceration of Père La Combe at, 145
Louville, M. de, *Memoirs*, 83-84
Louvois, 65, 67
Love, Pure, Doctrine of; *see "Amour pur"*
Loyola, Ignatius, and Ignatian system, 100-1, 116, 119, 125; *see also Spiritual Exercises*

Macaulay, Thomas Livingston, 43
Maintenon, Mme. de, 30, 35-39, 83, 167, 191, 198, 230; and Louis XIV, 31, 39 (marriage), 65, 75-76, 94, 163-64; and Fénelon, 35, 36-38, 41, 147, 148, 163, 164-65, 166, 175, 179, 185-87, 188-89, 190; and Mme. Guyon, 146-47, 148, 159, 167, 168, 169, 179, 186
Maisonfort, Mme. de, 146, 167, 199
Malebranche, 52-54 (Fénelon's *Refutation of M.'s Treatise on Nature and Grace*), 254
Marais, Paul Godet des, Bishop of Chartres; *see* Godet des Marais
Marie de'Medici, Queen, 94
Martin, Henri, 25, 97
Martineau, Père, letter from Fénelon to, on Duke of Burgundy, 85-86
Massacre of St. Bartholomew, 3, 28
Masson, P. M., 154, 245, 246
"Master Whimsical" (character in Fénelon's *Fables*), 81, 193
Maxims of the Saints (*Maximes des . . .*), Fénelon, 116, 187-88, 189, 192, 193, 194, 197, 226, 246
May, J. Lewis, 89
Meaux (bishopric of Bossuet), 54, 170; monuments associated with Bossuet at, 198-99

Meaux, Convent of the Visitation in, 178
"Meaux, Eagle of," name applied to Bossuet, 198
Meditations, Descartes, 93
Memorial, Pascal, 99
Mère Anne, of Carmelite Order, 123, 124
Molinos, Miguel de, 129, 130, 136, 144, 145, 169, 182; influence of writings, 131-132; trial and condemnation by Inquisition, 132; *see also, Spiritual Guide, The*
Montargis, 136-37, 142, 146; Benedictine convent in, 173, 174
Montaigne, 1, 253
Montbéron, Countess of: letter of Fénelon to, on St. François de Sales, 126-27; letters of spiritual counsel to, 239-42
Montespan, Mme. de, 38, 39, 75, 148
Montmorency-Laval, Marie Thérèse Françoise, Marquise de (cousin of Fénelon), 10, 50-51, 52
Motte, Jeanne Marie de la; *see* Guyon, Jeanne Marie de la Motte-
Motte, Père de la (brother of Jeanne), 137
Moyen court et facile de faire oraison, Mme. Guyon; *see Short and Easy Method of Prayer*
Music, Fénelon comments on, 61
Mystical Element in Religion, The, Baron von Hügel, 127-28, 193-94
Mysticism, Evelyn Underhill, 108, 115
Mysticism, Christian, 107-9; historically considered, 109-15; French, 17th century, 92, 93, 103-5, 116, 126, 127; Spanish contribution to, 117-18, 122-23; defined by Fénelon, 113-14; dangers in, 133-34; *see also* "Amour pur," doctrine of; Quakerism; Quietism; Illuminism
Mysticism, Christian, anonymous writings on; *see esp. Cloud of Unknowing, The*

[270]

Index

Index

Index